THE REAL READER'S QUARTERLY

Slightly Foxed

'An Unlikely Duo'

NO.54 SUMMER 2017

Editors: Gail Pirkis & Hazel Wood
Marketing and publicity: Stephanie Allen & Jennie Harrison Bunning
Bookshops: Anna Kirk
Subscriptions: Hattie Summers, Olivia Wilson & Katy Thomas

Cover fox: John Watson
Cover illustration: Oliver Akers Douglas, *The Avon at Salisbury*, oil on gesso panel

Oliver Akers Douglas, described by the critic Matthew Dennison as 'the foremost landscape painter of his generation', is best known for his dramatic interpretations of the English landscape. He works from life, using a Land Rover with a large easel welded to the side. His pictures vividly convey his experience of being on the spot, and the changing weather and light, and their surfaces are themselves textured landscapes of pure pigment. Beyond the process of manipulating paint, he is also concerned with the formal aspects of picture construction, conveying a three-dimensional experience in two-dimensional terms. Oliver is represented by Portland Gallery: www.portlandgallery.com.

Design by Octavius Murray

Layout by Andrew Evans

Colophon and tailpiece by David Eccles

Published by Slightly Foxed Limited
53 Hoxton Square
London N1 6PB

tel 020 7033 0258
fax 0870 1991245
email all@foxedquarterly.com
www.foxedquarterly.com

Slightly Foxed is published quarterly in early March, June, September and December

Annual subscription rates (4 issues)
UK and Ireland £40; Overseas £48

Single copies of this issue can be bought for £11 (UK) or £13 (Overseas)

All back issues in printed form are also available

ISBN 978-1-910898-02-4
ISSN 1742-5794

Printed and bound by Smith Settle, Yeadon, West Yorkshire

Contents

Contents

John Watson

For the digital edition of *Slightly Foxed* and an up-to-date list of partners and membership benefits, please visit the members' page on our website: www.foxedquarterly.com/members or contact Olivia: oliviawilson@foxedquarterly.com • +44 (0) 20 7033 0258

The Slightly Foxed office can obtain all books reviewed in this issue, whether new or second-hand. Please contact Anna: annakirk@foxedquarterly.com • +44 (0) 20 7033 0258

From the Editors

The trees are in full deep green leaf now, making a small oasis of Hoxton Square, while not fifty yards away the traffic roars past along Old Street. New regulations to cut down air pollution in London are on the way we learn, but now the fumes hang heavily in the summer air as we make for the office, dodging people coming in the other direction who seem to be talking to themselves but are actually on their mobile phones. As Jane Austen's great hypochondriac Mr Woodhouse observes, 'Nobody is healthy in London, nobody can be.' For many of us these days it's a hurrying, worrying world.

Here in the office however, against all the odds, we're well and in excellent spirits – but how badly sometimes one feels the need to escape, if only in the imagination, to a place where the pace is slower, the view more tranquil and more concentrated – the kind of country world that still existed when Adrian Bell wrote *The Cherry Tree*, a book which transports you to another England, still recognizable yet remote.

This newest of the Slightly Foxed Editions is the third and last volume in a trilogy of lightly fictionalized memoirs in which Bell describes his experiences of leaving London in the decade after the First World War to work on a Suffolk farm. In the first two, *Corduroy* and *Silver Ley* (see *SF* nos. 22 and 46) he learns farming on a well-established family farm near Bury St Edmunds and acquires a small farm of his own; in *The Cherry Tree* (see p.14) he marries and settles down to sit out the agricultural depression of the late Twenties and Thirties as best he can. The books are a wonderfully poetic and detailed record of a time in the countryside before mechanization took over completely and when many of the old crafts and their colourful practitioners still survived. They are books that have been loved since they were first published in the 1930s, and they still resonate today.

On the subject of books with lasting qualities, on p.42 you'll find an interview with the prize-winning novelist and playwright Ali Smith. Maggie Fergusson went to Cambridge to meet her and talk about the way she approaches her work and deals with the many demands which are made on successful writers in this media age. It's the first in a new occasional series on living authors who are still writing and who have a considerable body of work behind them which we feel will last. We hope you'll enjoy it and welcome any suggestions you may have for additions to the series.

For anyone with a busy life, or indeed an inner life, a good notebook, we feel, is essential – a place for lifesaving lists, memorable quotes and titles of interesting books you've read about, a repository for Great Thoughts and acute passing observations for that novel you plan. Many of you clearly agree, for our Slightly Foxed notebooks, which we introduced a couple of years ago at the suggestion of our contributor James Roose-Evans, have shot off the shelves. We have a new batch in now in a different range of colours: a smart charcoal, a fresh apple green and a distinguished maroon, as well as our signature duck-egg blue. Bound in coloured cloth with contrasting endpapers, silk head- and tailband and ribbon marker, they come in two sizes, one identical to the Slightly Foxed Editions and one the same size as the quarterly itself. The good-quality paper is unruled, so they can serve equally well as both notebooks and sketchbooks. Perfect for taking on holiday.

And finally, as always we're enjoying planning our annual Readers' Day at the Art Workers' Guild in Bloomsbury, which this year is on Saturday, 4 November. Tickets are now available and you'll find more details on p. 93. See you there we hope.

GAIL PIRKIS & HAZEL WOOD

An Unlikely Duo

YSENDA MAXTONE GRAHAM

Is it acceptable to be both happily married to a living man and physically attracted to a long-dead author? I know I'm not the only one. I have one friend who goes weak at the knees when she shows me photos of the late Patrick Leigh Fermor, and another who has a lasting physical pash for Joseph Banks (1743–1820). Mine is for Peter Fleming (1907–71), older brother of Ian.

The good thing about being in love with a dead person is that you can't be unfaithful; nor can you feel too jealous of the person's love affairs with other people. On the contrary, it's almost a pleasure to luxuriate in imagining those love affairs. So I think: lucky, lucky Celia Johnson! In real life, the man who adored her was not Trevor Howard of *Brief Encounter* but Peter Fleming of the joyously laughing smile, the sinewy forearms and the sublime prose. While Fleming was halfway through the seven-month journey from Peking to India in 1935 that he would immortalize in *News from Tartary*, Celia received a letter from him that included the words, 'My darling Celia, whom I love . . .' I like to imagine her opening the envelope and reading and rereading those words, in *his* handwriting.

I also derive a guilty pleasure from luxuriating in the fact that Fleming was very much *not* in love with the rather masculine woman he was travelling with on that journey – the woman who would also immortalize it, in her book *Forbidden Journey*. That woman was

---

Peter Fleming, *News from Tartary* (1936) · I. B. Tauris · Pb · 424pp · £12.99 · ISBN 9781780765037; Ella Maillart, *Forbidden Journey* (1937), is out of print but we can obtain second-hand copies.

Ella Maillart (1903–97), nicknamed Kini, an international skier and Olympic sailor who also played hockey for Switzerland. The two had met in 1934 when they found themselves drinking beer together in a London nightclub; Kini had casually asked Fleming, 'How do I get into the Soviet Republic in South China?' and Fleming had replied, 'You don't.' The exchange turned out to be the catalyst for embarking on a journey together to prove the statement false.

When Fleming introduces Kini in *News from Tartary*, he describes her as 'tall, rather good-looking, with a brown face and fair hair'. Not 'very good-looking' or even plain 'good-looking'. 'Rather good-looking' is brutal, a scarcely veiled euphemism for 'unattractive and looks like a man'. Did Kini's heart sink when she read that description? Fleming was even more open about his lack of attraction to her in a letter to his friend Rupert Hart-Davis, quoted in the biography of Fleming written by Duff Hart-Davis and published while Kini was still alive: 'The Swiss is bearing up well, and we remain on speaking though not always in my case on listening terms; she is an honest soul and quite useful.' But, 'As far as the Affections go, she will never mean more to me than a yak.'

But, strangely, it worked. The two intrepid travellers were united in their determination to complete the journey. 'When we got to Peking,' Fleming writes, 'it was at once apparent that the chances of reaching India overland were infinitesimal.' To do so required passing through Sinkiang (now Xinjiang), a vast province that had been cut off from the rest of China since the civil war of 1934, during which the Soviets had taken over, pushing out the Tungan (Chinese Mongol) rebels. Any European who had tried to enter Sinkiang in the past year had either been imprisoned or murdered. Fleming wanted to find out exactly what was going on in Sinkiang and to write about it for *The Times*, before publishing it in book form. But would he and Maillart be allowed in, and once in, out? On every page, the dread of being sent back is palpable. But border officials everywhere seemed to turn to putty when confronted with Fleming's Etonian charm.

Setting out on a ride of 3,500 miles, Fleming writes, is 'like sitting down to read *The Faerie Queene* right through, only worse'. We've all tried that, so we know what he means. Travelling on bucking pony, on bony camel, on ignoble donkey and on tired foot, sometimes with just a guide, sometimes as part of a huge Mongol caravan, they edge their way round the vast salty lake of Koko Nor, and across thousands of miles of the Tsaidam marshes and the Taklamakan desert. Depending on the weather, the scene looks like either 'a couple of chapters out of Exodus' or 'the Retreat from Moscow'. As with Tolkien, the reader lives every minute of the desolation, empathizing with the exhausted load-bearing beasts, and relishing the longed-for arrivals in friendly villages, even if some of them turn out to be no more than half a dozen dilapidated yurts. When Fleming and Maillart eventually lumber into Kashgar, in the far west of Sinkiang, they discover they've been officially reported as missing.

Kini talks a lot, and sometimes she yodels. At a happy moment on the journey she writes, 'I could have shouted for joy, and the echoes rang with my Alpine songs.' Oh, Kini, how I feel for you! You shared a tent with Peter for months, crossing thousands of miles of desert *à deux*, washing your faces in the frying-pan; he let you use his gun-cleaning rod as a skewer to cook the meat he'd shot; you mended his clothes and cooked him a delicious curry on his twenty-eighth birthday; he was utterly charming to you throughout the journey; but the only time he laid hands on you was when he massaged you to soothe your lumbago. The only times you touched him – I counted – were (1) when you caught him and saved his life when he nearly fell out of a lorry, (2) when he asked you to give him a haircut, and (3) at this moment in the middle of the Taklamakan desert:

> In the middle of the night I woke with a start and in the darkness made out the head of a baby camel resting on my knees. I could not believe my eyes and put my hand out to stroke the woolly head. But it proved to be Peter's hair.

That is a poignant moment: poignant, because it becomes clear in Maillart's account that she is a solitary and rather unloved soul. While Peter chafes at any delay, impatient to stride homewards as fast as possible to his life of popularity as an acclaimed *Times* writer – and to get back to Scotland in time for the grouse season – Kini writes: 'I wanted to forget that we had inevitably to return home . . . I should have liked the journey to continue for the rest of my life.' We glimpse her isolation when, after six months of travelling, with no communication whatsoever from home, they meet some Swedish missionaries.

> They said [wrote Peter] that there was a telegram waiting for me at Gilgit, and this news – for I am a kind of specialist in anticipation – was almost better than receiving the telegram itself.

There was indeed a telegram waiting for him, as well as a pile of letters – but there was no mail at all for Kini.

Did Peter let on to Kini that he had a glamorous actress girlfriend back in London? I don't think he did. Celia Johnson certainly had no idea that Peter was travelling with another woman. He had teased Celia the previous year, pretending to be smitten by a glamorous Swiss international skier – and he could not bring himself to admit that he was now travelling, albeit platonically, with that very woman, let alone sleeping in the same tent. So we have the complicated telegram he wrote to Hart-Davis just before his return: 'DUE MONDAY DEBAG SWISS CAT IF CELIAS COMING CROYDON.' In other words, 'Let the cat out of the bag to Celia that I've been travelling alone with another woman for the past seven months.'

As you will have gathered, while other people might read the two accounts of the journey as pure travel books, I read them as gripping psychological dramas in which both writers betray more than they mean to about their inner lives.

It's accepted wisdom that Fleming's *News from Tartary*, published in 1936, is the classic and readable account of the journey, and that Ella Maillart's account (first published in French in 1937 as *Oasis interdites*) is the boring one. *News from Tartary* was a runaway best-seller; *Forbidden Journey* was only a modest success. Again, poor Kini! Her informative, carefully descriptive prose doesn't have a chance against the verbal acrobatics of Fleming. He would never use (as Maillart does) classic travel-book expressions such as 'Legend has it' or 'As if we had not troubles enough'. He would never (as Maillart does) begin a sentence with the history-lesson phrase, 'In the eleventh century'. Nor would he ever (as she does) actually *say* that something was funny. Instead, he concocts perfectly formed sentences like this one, describing a hair-raising downhill lorry journey:

> The Chinese, either ignorant of or impatient with the orthodox sign-vocabulary, declined on their notice-boards to commit themselves to the exact nature of the peril in wait for the motorist, and merely painted a bold and arresting exclamation mark. As we hurtled downwards the recurrent '!' atoned for its inadequacy as a warning by its charming aptness as a comment.

And this one, about a desolate village called Dzunchia that 'looked, felt and smelt like the end of the world':

> The desert is clean and comfortable, and the Ritz is clean and comfortable; it is on the first of the stages from the desert to the Ritz that you find the real dirt, the real discomfort.

And this one, summing up another hopeless Chinese village:

> As we arrived at the inn, the building next to it . . . quietly and rather sadly collapsed, crumbling to rubble in a cloud of dust. It was one of those days.

Every paragraph contains a gem or two of comic observation like those; Fleming can't write without being funny about absolutely everything.

Reading the two accounts in succession, though, I came to like Maillart's more serious and less show-offy way of describing things. Fleming's book, in a way, is *about* his prose. He revels in his desire not to bore us, or himself, with too many facts or Chinese words: at the forefront of his mind, I think, was the desire to make the editor of *The Times* roar with laughter. 'The politics of Asia', he writes, 'are richly encrusted with polysyllables scarcely pronounceable, and so similar in their outlandish unfamiliarity that the ordinary reader has the greatest difficulty in distinguishing between a place, a political leader, and a prevailing wind.'

Maillart's prose is a window on the journey, and nothing more or less. She does occasionally bore us, dividing her chapters up with dreary sub-headings such as 'Religious Cross-Roads' and 'The Gorges of the Altyn Tagh'. She's fascinated by the political situation in China, cares deeply about it, and wants us to care too. She notices women with bound feet, and maltreated animals, and describes them with great compassion. Whenever she and Peter arrive at a village, the locals crowd round and ask her to cure them of their various illnesses, and she gets out her medicine chest and does her best. When she begins sentences with 'I caused much hilarity . . .' that's a sure sign that what she's about to write is not going to make us laugh. But there's more to life than hilarity. I felt for her when she wrote: 'In his imperturbable wisdom Peter looked on human beings as characters in a comedy. He was bored by my craving to understand the thousands of diverse lives that make up humanity.'

Both carried Leica cameras, and both books are full of evocative photographs. Peter's photographs are a *comédie humaine* of stock characters whose antics he has nailed; Kini's bring out the kindness and sweetness of the people they met.

Fleming boldly devotes a whole chapter to describing how the two of them got on. 'By all the conventions of desert island fiction,' he writes, 'we should have fallen madly in love with each other; by all the laws of human nature we should have driven each other crazy

with irritation. As it was, we missed these almost equally embarrassing alternatives by a wide margin.' It's a touching chapter, expressing the genuine respect and liking they felt for each other. Kini's book has no such chapter; but she does occasionally let rip: 'Peter returned from his hunting, happy at having had a good day while I minded the house.' Or 'I made no bones about telling Peter what I thought of people who travelled too fast and took no time to learn anything about anything.'

I gaze at the final photograph of them at the end of *Forbidden Journey*, captioned: 'Delhi: the expedition breaks up.' They're side by side on the tarmac at the airport, smartened up, Peter thin and smiling with a pipe clamped between his teeth, Kini also smiling and wearing a skirt after months in trousers. They're about to go their separate ways: Peter to be blissfully reunited with Celia, whom he would soon marry; Kini to go home to a life of spinsterhood.

'On the road,' Peter writes, 'we had, I think, found much the same kind of happiness in much the same kind of things; and I would have liked the end of the road to have given us both equal pleasure.'

YSENDA MAXTONE GRAHAM's grandparents had Peter and Celia Fleming to supper in Chelsea in the 1930s, the lucky things. Ysenda's latest book, *Terms & Conditions: Life in Girls' Boarding Schools, 1939–1979*, is available from Slightly Foxed.

Ploughing On

HAZEL WOOD

The writer Adrian Bell first arrived in Suffolk in 1920 – a delicate young would-be poet, fresh from public school at Uppingham and the polite drawing-rooms of Chelsea, under pressure from his father, who was news editor of the *Observer*, to get a proper job. He was, he says, 'flying from the threat of office life' when he first presented himself for work on the farm of an old-established farming family in the countryside near Bury St Edmunds.

At first Bell made the townie's mistake of assuming that country people were a fairly simple lot, but he soon thought differently. In this new world, he was the one who seemed unfit and incompetent. But he was a quick learner and a passion for the land took hold of him. He settled in Suffolk, and farmed for the rest of his life, recording those early days almost as he lived them in a trilogy of lightly fictionalized memoirs, the first two, *Corduroy* and *Silver Ley*, published in 1930 and 1931 (see *SF* nos. 22 and 46) and the third, *The Cherry Tree*, in 1932.

Bell may never have been recognized as a poet, but in these books his keen and sympathetic eye combined with the practicality of the farmer to create some of the most poetic yet down-to-earth accounts ever written of life in the English countryside in those last days before mechanization took over completely. They were the books that soldiers slipped into their kitbags when they went to war in 1939 to remind them of the life that many of them had left behind. They have been favourites of mine ever since I read the first of them in a cottage looking out on the same flat East Anglian fields and wide horizons that Adrian Bell came to love.

By the time *The Cherry Tree* opens Bell is established on his own small farm, Silver Ley, not far from Bury St Edmunds (which he calls Stambury). But although by this time he has grown to enjoy the life and its independence, the farmhouse has begun to seem rather a cold place in the evenings when he comes in tired to a dead fire and a lonely supper. Almost to persuade himself that all this hard labour has been worthwhile, he starts setting down on paper memories of his early days in Suffolk, and the publication of this first book in the trilogy leads to an unexpected fan letter from a young woman called Nora (in real life her name was Marjorie) whom he eventually meets and marries.

In her letter Nora tells him she has enjoyed *Corduroy* because the life described in it 'seemed like clean linen, shining forks and spoons, the beauty of everything you use every day'. It was, Bell says, 'continually with me, as I went about that morning, that such beauty, the bright-worn, manual workaday beauty of what one used, was the light of life to me, though it had not occurred to me in those words'.

In fact I can't think of a more apt way to convey the charm of these books. The world they capture – so different from the one in which many of us now live, or partly live – is a tactile one, in which knowledge and experience come through making, using, doing; where the craftsman takes pride not only in the quality and usefulness of what he has made but in its beauty too. Here is old Mark Ashen, the wheelwright, choosing wood for the cart he is going to make for Bell at a time when such beautifully made carts were beginning to go out of fashion.

> I went into his wood-store with him to select the timber for my tumbril. He smoothed his hand along one plank and another, murmuring 'Now that's a lovely piece of wood – that came out of Creevely Park in Lord Wenford's time.' And he talked with his hand resting flat upon it as if it were a source of strength. He rolled the great tree-sections about like the segments of a shat-

tered pillar, choosing two that should do for the hubs. We chose the axle-tree and the shafts. I think he felt that he would not have the opportunity of using much more of his plentiful store which father laid up for son . . .

And the old man not only makes and paints the cart, but proudly decorates it too, with Bell's name and address, and innumerable delicately painted flourishes and small motifs, so that when Darkie the horse drew it out of Mark Ashen's yard 'it was as though a king had departed'.

Some of these small cameos of life in this then remote part of East Anglia seem bathed in the mellow light of an old painting. There is a description of Charlie Todd, the overseer of the great barn on a neighbour's farm, meticulously preparing the space for threshing. There is enormous pride and authority in the way he does his job, and a painterly eye in Bell's depiction of it and of the great barn itself:

> There was a wooden dais at one end, on either side of which the beams rose and curved ruggedly to the roof . . . a small door opened from half-way up on one side, through which sheaves had once been pushed at harvest-time. I have seen the sun coming through this opening in a single shaft, striking down upon the dais, a sloping pillar of haze. One was aware suddenly of the emptiness of the place, and of a presage and concentration, as though light were mind. One waited for the first actor in some old play to enter and halt there and speak his prologue.

This farm is well-run and well-established, but farming life is changing – 'the old bluff hospitable life of the countryside' as Bell calls it, with its well-peopled farms, its hunting and shooting and generous sociability, is passing. Economic depression means that few can now afford these luxuries. Farmers are giving up, and there is a wrenching description of the bankruptcy of an old neighbour turned off his farm, who at the last cannot bear to be parted from his one cow, Daisy. Finally he asks Bell to take her and Bell buys her from him, but 'for another week he hung about the gate of the meadow where Daisy was . . . When I passed he'd say again, "I'd as lief you had her as anybody."'

Poultry, which had once been a sideline for the farmer's wife, is now becoming a vital part of the farm's economy, and broiler houses are springing up. The heavy hand of bureaucracy is beginning to be felt, with visits from the Government Inspector, sent to look at Bell's milking and butter-making arrangements, which are found to be wanting, and his weights and measures, which are rejected because they are not 'Government stamped'. Yet despite it all Bell feels that a hard life in the country is preferable to what he sees as the hectic and debased life of the city with its 'modernity neurosis', and he decides to hang on and wait for better times.

As well as evoking the period and the way of life of Bell's country neighbours, *The Cherry Tree* is also a picture of a new marriage. In the conservative terms of the farming community the Bells are a somewhat unconventional couple, for Nora, though charming, kind and capable, is also quietly determined and independent-minded. She likes to accompany Bell and his farmer friend Bob Chilgrove on their walks round the farm, whereas normally wives stay in the house and 'talk domestic matters'. She even helps in the fields, planting potatoes – and she doesn't wear a hat! It's clearly a marriage of equals, but Bell is certain that the village's verdict on them is 'She rule he, that's a fact.'

Despite all the hardships, the picture is a happy one, and *The Cherry Tree* is a cheerful book written by a young and happy man. Later the couple would have three children – the translator Anthea Bell, best known for her English translations of *Asterix*, and the twins Sylvia and Martin, the former war reporter and independent MP.

Adrian Bell himself went on to write twenty more books on the countryside and from 1950 wrote the 'Countryman's Notes' column for the *Eastern Daily Press*. He was a friend of the painter John Nash and together they collaborated on *Men and the Fields*, published in 1939, a poignant record in words and pictures of the Stour Valley countryside between the Bells' farmhouse and Nash's house at Bottengom's Farm, which is now the home of the writer Ronald Blythe. When in 1930 the *Daily Telegraph*'s new daily crossword started attracting readers away from *The Times*, Bell's father suggested him for the job – Bell had never even solved a crossword before and had only ten days to work out the first – and between then and 1978 he set around 5,000 *Times* crosswords, establishing the paper's distinctive 'cryptic' style.

In one of the final chapters of *The Cherry Tree* a fair comes to the village and Bell describes how the laughter and loud music and the heady feeling of irresponsibility it brings give him a sense of regret at 'how careful I had grown in the cultivation of the earth, how content with felicity and shrunken in ambition'. Yet he was simultaneously uplifted, 'excited again by the dream that there was something in life that I alone knew, which I alone could tell'. It was in fact that slow, observant 'cultivation of the earth' that spoke through Bell's writing, giving depth and substance to his wonderful trilogy – a lasting story of this countryside and its people that 'he alone could tell'.

HAZEL WOOD is a Devonian who has lived in London for forty years but still dreams of living in East Anglia.

Strunking It

NIGEL JARRETT

I took to E. B. White, author of *Charlotte's Web* and other books for children and grown-ups with Peter Pan tendencies, when he wrote that New York reached its highest point architecturally when at its lowest economically. That was from an essay called 'Here Is New York' and it seemed to me typical of a New Yorker's choice turn of phrase; that's to say, the phrase of a dweller in that city who also worked for the magazine of the same name and who wouldn't turn any phrase until it were guaranteed to pass muster in front of its famously scrupulous fact-checkers. They checked grammar as well as facts and were also strict about the way ideas were expressed. White was doubly endowed, for he both wrote checked copy and checked the copy of others. That he could scarcely risk committing a bare solecism was down to William Strunk Jr., who led an English course at Cornell University when White was a student there. White graduated from his class and never forgot him.

More accurately, he never forgot Strunk's book. Strunk had written a slim volume called *The Elements of Style*, which became the course's set text. White was so impressed with it that thirty-eight years later, in 1957, he accepted a commission from Macmillan to revise it for the college market and the general trade, by which was meant students who even then could embark on a university course with only a rudimentary grasp of English, and anyone else who needed to communicate in an increasingly voluble world. Strunk had

---

William Strunk Jr. and E. B. White, *The Elements of Style* (4th edition, 1999), is out of print but second-hand copies are readily available.

argued for affirmation, cleanliness, accuracy, and brevity in the use of language. White revised the book again in 1971, when he thought its vigour unimpaired. My copy, a *vade mecum*, is a 1979 reprint.

It strikes me that in just a couple of paragraphs I've been too liberal with adverbs, which would have raised a Strunk eyebrow. Also, that comma after the word 'accuracy' is an example of White applying a Strunk rule concerning the 'serial' comma: *In a series of three or more terms with a single conjunction, use a comma after each term except the last.* This is rule No. 2 in Strunk's Elementary Rules of Usage. It's not what I was taught in school but then, my English teachers appeared to make up the rules as they went along, if they applied them at all. To this platoon of easy-going pedagogues I make an exception for Major W. H. Wood, who took me for O-level English and introduced me to box analysis, an exercise in giving a name to every word of a sentence on pain of extending the school day. I enjoyed the exercise, if few of my schoolmates did. Rules of English were what amounted to consensus in published books, their provenance having been clouded by Time's enveloping mist. To grasp them, one had to read and read widely and often. Rules were absorbed unconsciously. (Oh dear; more adverbs.)

The problem for a writer like White when stepping into the stylist's domain is the need to obey the rules he's about to consider. He confined his revision of Strunk's manual to the addition of a chapter that included his own 'notions of error', perhaps realizing that Strunk's unequivocal commands – Do this, Don't do that – did not reflect the idea of language, any language, as something evolving. What neither of them would countenance, though, was the perpetration of errors that confounded linguistic sense, even when widely committed. This is covered at its most basic in Strunk's list of words commonly misused. They would have agreed that application of Strunkian certainties was not a competition in which what the majority thought was, *ipso facto*, correct, but there is always a sense in which inflexible sticklers for the rules among grammarians are tidally challenged Canutes. Strunk insisted that the word 'try' should always take the infinitive: 'try to', not 'try and'. He says,

> Students of the language will argue that *try and* has won through and become idiom. Indeed it has, and it is relaxed and acceptable. But *try to* is precise, and when you are writing formal prose, try and write *try to*.

One feels that Strunk gave in to these small defeats with more resignation than regret.

Most of Strunk's injunctions repeat common and commonsense rules of grammar and syntax, though his hatred of the term 'student body' and his preference for 'studentry' after the example of 'citizenry' shows how usage is often personal and sometimes eccentric. His revulsion for the expression 'the fact that' was legendary. 'It should be revised out of every sentence in which it occurs,' he fumed. But White comments that 'a shadow of gloom' seemed to hang over the page and one felt that Strunk knew how hopeless his cause sometimes was. Indeed, both Strunk and White eschewed inflexibility and warned against the danger of doctrine. White's revisionist chapter, a classic of maintaining almost to the letter the standards espoused in the book he was adding to, is an exegesis of that precept.

A former journalist, I collect newspaper style books. Most of them simply lay down rules of consistency: if there's more than one way of spelling a word, let it be the same every time. Keith Waterhouse, a former *Daily Mirror* journalist, wrote two excellent books of the Strunk sort, though at greater length and in an obvious attempt to curb the popular newspaper journalist's excesses, particularly by removing cliché and discouraging exaggeration. My own (provincial) newspaper's style book – or stylebook, as it insisted – included a few Strunk-like do's and don'ts, including the rule that 'do's and don'ts' should be written that way on the grounds that 'dos' as a plural simply didn't look right. Like other style books, its idea of continuity had no empirical foundation. Nor was the word 'nonet' likely to appear in its columns, even though, and I quote, it had to be 'nonet not nonette'.

I have two prose books by White: a collection of his essays and a selection of other pieces – long, short, and often whimsical – from *The New Yorker*. It's a sad reflection on my reading of them that I am constantly looking for deployments that would have disappointed his mentor. I have found none. *The Elements of Style* should be posted through every letterbox in the land. Or should that be letter-box?

NIGEL JARRETT once 'subbed' for a daily newspaper, attempting without much enthusiasm to apply the rules of its often bizarre style book. He's a winner of the Rhys Davies Award for short fiction and the author, so far, of a book of stories, a poetry collection and a novel.

Once a Catholic . . .

MELISSA HARRISON

There it is on my shelf, that familiar bottle-green spine – the first in a quartet by the same author. This quartet has shadowed me for twenty-two years now: to various sets of university lodgings and back; to three dark rooms above a car dealership in Dalston, my first ever London flat; to two house-shares and then a bedsit in Clapham Junction; and now to Streatham, my home for the last dozen years. In all that time, though, I haven't opened any of them; in fact, all four spines remain uncracked.

As I reluctantly pick up the first – No. 1 in the Virago Modern Classics series – I realize that I've been avoiding rereading Antonia White's first novel, *Frost in May* (1933), for over half my life. Yet the teenage me would have told you it was one of my favourite books; why, then, has it become such a forbidding presence on my shelves? Inside, my mother's familiar handwriting ('From a proud Mum and Dad') brings a whisper of grief in its wake, but the truth is, that's not it. There are books that change you in unforgettable ways, that teach you things or make the world larger: books that help you grow. But there are books that hurt you, too, or haunt you. Such a book, for me, is *Frost in May*.

Antonia White was born Eirene Botting in London in 1899. Her father, a teacher, converted to Catholicism in 1906, and she and her mother were received into the Church at the same time. At 9 she was sent to the Convent of the Sacred Heart in Surrey, where many of

---

Antonia White, *Frost in May* (1933)
Virago · Pb · 224pp · £8.99 · ISBN 9781844083787

the other girls hailed from the old, aristocratic Catholic families of Europe. She was expelled on her fifteenth birthday, and it is those years, lightly fictionalized, that *Frost in May* describes.

My Virago edition, given to me by my parents in my second year at Oxford, includes a 1948 introduction by Elizabeth Bowen. It begins, '*Frost in May* is a girls' school story. It is not the only school story to be a classic; but I can think of no other that is a work of art.' It was, I suppose, *Frost in May*'s status as a 'school story' that led me to read it so early, for I can only have been 11 or 12 when I discovered a dog-eared copy on my parents' shelves, though I was too naïve then to be able to digest it properly.

Nanda Grey is 9 when she arrives, with her father, at the Convent of the Five Wounds, Lippington. She is met by the impenetrable and efficient Mother Radcliffe who sweeps towards her down a chilly corridor and asks whether she will say goodbye to her father straight away, or sit with him for a little in the parlour.

'What do you think, Nanda? It's late and Mother will be waiting. But I'll stay if you like,' Mr Grey says.

> 'It's all right, Daddy,' said Nanda mechanically. She suddenly felt lonely and frightened. A great longing came over her for small shabby rooms and coal fires and the comfortable smells of tobacco and buttered toast. But she was one of those children who cannot help behaving well.

This is such a delicately written scene. Her father makes his wish to leave clear but veils it with a cursory offer to stay; she responds to the hidden message just as her parents have trained her, immediately subsuming her own wishes and fears. This is 'behaving well'.

Within moments of her father leaving, Nanda is humiliated for the first time when she makes the sign of the cross with her left hand instead of her right. It is not the ignorance of a recent convert that leads her into error, but politeness: for Mother Radcliffe is holding her right hand. There is great skill in the way White allows the reader to observe these injustices without overtly drawing our attention to them: four pages in and we are already experiencing the world through Nanda's 9-year-old eyes, for whom Father is irreproachable and Mother Radcliffe tactful and kind.

The convent at Lippington is drawn with beguiling exactness – the smell of beeswax in the corridors, the 'exemptions' and coloured ribbons that form its mysterious system of rewards, the other girls with their ponies and holy pictures, 'the stewed meat and rice, cabbage drowned in vinegar, and sweet tea . . . poured from enormous metal urns'. It is an airless world in which the girls' friendships are constantly spied upon, their most harmless transgressions punished in ways that seem unarguable because they are given the backing of a monolithic religion. Rereading *Frost in May* as an adult, the nuns' cruelty and snobbery seem starkly clear; but the book's power comes from the way in which it depicts austere Lippington – and the particular strain of Catholicism practised there – as both glamorous and, in an obscure way, safe: 'You Catholics are wonderfully definite about everything, aren't you? It must be a great comfort to know just where one is,' says a Protestant girl, Clare, to Nanda at one point. To me at 11, both the moral certainty and the new language of retreats and indulgences, saints and vocations, held an extremely powerful allure.

When Nanda has been at Lippington for five days her parents visit.

> She was on the point of skating recklessly over the waxed floor to fling herself upon them, when someone laid a restraining arm on her sleeve. It was the nun in charge of the parlour. At Lippington one did not meet even one's nearest relatives without surveillance.

Nanda curtseys to her parents instead, something for which her father praises her: 'I felt quite like a French aristocrat coming to see his beautiful young daughter,' he says, revealingly. The school is full of aristocrats, but the Greys are certainly not among them.

> 'I *never* saw a place with so many rules and regulations,' wailed Mrs Grey. 'I'm sure we waited at *least* half an hour for you, darling child, didn't we, John?'
>
> 'Several minutes, certainly,' said Mr Grey, 'but I expect Nanda was a long way away.'
>
> 'Yes,' said Nanda spotlessly, 'and I had to do my hair and put on my gloves.' She felt remote and self-possessed.

How chilling is that 'spotlessly', for Nanda is indeed a very long way away. Already the world of the convent is closing over her head.

Her parents leave her with a book, *Dream Days* by Kenneth Grahame, to give as a birthday present to Marjorie Appleyard, a girl the family knows slightly but whom Nanda does not even like. It is discovered by Mother Frances, and confiscated – and Nanda loses her 'exemption' as punishment: 'We do not encourage particular friendships among little girls,' she is told. And there's a further slight: 'The tone of this book is not at all the kind of thing we like at Lippington. Apart from its being by a non-Catholic writer, it is morbid, rather unwholesome, and just a *little* vulgar,' the nun says.

Yet just a few years later, when she is in the senior school, Mother Radcliffe instructs Nanda to cultivate the society of girls 'of her station in life' such as Marjorie, rather than her close friends Rosario de Palencia and Léonie Magdalena Hedwig de Wesseldorf: 'Conversion is a great grace, but the Catholic outlook, Catholic breeding, shall we say, does not come in one generation, or even two, or three.' It is clear that despite all her efforts Nanda will never be accepted, never fully fit in.

What could save Nanda from the systematic damage that is being inflicted on her is a strong sense of selfhood and a knowledge that she is essentially good – what Mother Radcliffe terms 'a hard little core of self-will and self-love'. But it is exactly this that the nuns want to extinguish, and they are explicit about it, too. 'Do you know that no character is any good in this world unless that will has been broken completely? Broken and re-set in God's own way,' Mother Frances tells her after a minor infraction. 'I don't think your will has quite been broken, my dear child, do you?' And so they set about it. To reveal their final method would be to spoil the book's ending; suffice to say that the deliberate injustice of the circumstances surrounding Nanda's removal from the school – circumstances which mirrored White's own – horrified me at 11, and still horrifies me now.

To be moved by *Frost in May* is natural; but why the powerful mixture of adoration and aversion that has marked my thirty-year relationship with the book? Nanda is a clever, imaginative child from a comparatively hard-up family – as I was. She is close to her father, who is proud of her intelligence, but she finds her mother irritating and over-emotional, and clear fault-lines at home have caused her to develop coping mechanisms that will not serve her well. She finds it hard to fit in at school, as I did, and is openly disliked by some teachers for her precociousness. She is an only child, whereas I was the youngest of six; but with a large gap between me and my older siblings I did much of my growing-up alone. Yet it is only when returning to *Frost in May* now, with great trepidation, that I can see the parallels between us; for me as a little girl, the 1930s setting, Nanda's only-child status and the exoticism of the convent school meant that – consciously at least – I failed to see myself in her. All I knew then was that I was entranced by it all, to the extent that for a decade or so the thought nagged at me that perhaps – although barely even a churchgoer – I should convert. This is strange, to say the least, given that Catholic doctrine is one of the weapons the nuns deploy so terrifyingly in the book.

With the passage of time I've come to understand that lonely, bullied children often blame themselves for their rejection, because it preserves the belief that if they change enough, they'll one day fit in. My childish desire to become a Catholic was not religious conviction, but a reaction to the terrifying spectre of exclusion White conjured, which had found such an echo in me. Had I first read *Frost in May* in my twenties I would have seen Lippington for the abusive establishment that it was, and understood that what happened to Nanda wasn't her fault; at 11 I believed at some confused level that I might succeed where she had failed.

It would take fifteen years and a complete mental breakdown, followed by years of therapy, before White was able to complete her second book, *The Lost Traveller* (1950), and to follow that with *The Sugar House* (1952) and *Beyond the Glass* (1954). Although the main character's name in those three books is Clara Batchelor, they are again semi-autobiographical, and together with *Frost in May* they describe the difficult course of White's own early life.

White became a copywriter and an award-winning translator of, among other books, Colette's *Claudine* novels and Guy de Maupassant's *Une Vie*. She married three times and had two daughters, both of whom have written memoirs describing their treatment at her hands ('Man hands on misery to man,' as Larkin said). Unsurprisingly her early experiences cost her her faith, although she recovered it in 1940; but the damage the Convent of the Sacred Heart did to her was deeper than that, and proved irreparable. As she explained in *The Book of Catholic Authors* in 1942, '"creative joy" is something I haven't felt since I was fourteen and don't expect to feel again'.

MELISSA HARRISON's most recent novel, *At Hawthorn Time*, was longlisted for the Baileys Women's Prize for Fiction and shortlisted for the Costa Novel Award. An atheist, she has no plans to write a memoir of her days at a comprehensive school.

Up on the Down

COLIN WILLIAMS

Six years ago when we moved into our neglected nineteenth-century house on the edge of Hampshire's chalk downs it was a move into two worlds. One was of damp walls, dangerously amateur wiring, a wheezing boiler and icy, see-your-own-breath bedrooms. The other was of the world that lay beyond the streaming window-panes, the sea of rolling green turf that filled the view on two sides from our position in the valley – Watership Down.

Richard Adams's first and far and away most successful book was published in 1972 but it feels as if it's been with us for much longer, so established is it now in the list of childhood classics. Originating in the stories Adams told his children to lighten the boredom of long car journeys, *Watership Down* is a simple tale, but one with epic and universal themes: an arduous and dangerous journey, near-death encounters, doubts over a self-imposed exile from a lost homeland, loss of innocence and the search for peace; a peace that would eventually be found – as it has been for us – on Watership Down.

Walking along the old drover's road to the top of the down I sometimes see and hear the rabbits that are the heroes of the book, all bustle and haste on the dark edges of the beech hangers. Carry on past coppiced woods and path verges knee-deep in cow parsley and you emerge blinking on to the bright and open down itself. This is

---

Richard Adams, *Watership Down* (1972)
Puffin · Pb · 656pp · £6.99 · ISBN 9780141354965

where the rabbits' journey comes to an end, but the journey begins with a febrile, terrifying vision.

It is late springtime, five miles to the north on Sandleford Common – easily visible across farmland and copses – where the story begins. Fiver, a rabbit-prophet of sorts, sits before a man-made sign. 'This is where it comes from!' he tells his brother Hazel. 'There isn't any danger here, at this moment. But it's coming – it's coming. Oh, Hazel, look! The field! It's covered with blood!'

Though he doesn't understand the words on the sign, Fiver has sensed the death and destruction the threatened housing development will bring, and the choking gas that will be used to clear their warren. The next evening, scorned by his elders as fanciful and power-hungry, Fiver leaves the warren with Hazel and eleven other rabbits. They strike southwards, inspired by Fiver's vision of a safe haven, green, abundant and secure, high above the fields of their ancestors.

For speed and safety, most of the rabbits' journey takes place under cover of darkness, along the edge-lands of farms and fields and in the shade of cool burrows. Danger lies in bright daylight and open ground. Before long they believe they've found safe haven when they meet a sleek and healthy rabbit called Cowslip. He is part of a warren that at first appears to offer abundance, goodwill and protection from *elil*, the rabbits' term for the creatures that prey on them. But it's Fiver the seer, whose 'horrors kept him above ground all night in the rain, oblivious of old and prowling *elil*', who sees the danger in the vegetable roots and scraps the nearby farmer leaves for the well-fed rabbits. He is vindicated when the redoubtable Bigwig is caught in a shiny-wired snare. Faced with a thrashing, struggling rabbit, throat half cut, the others realize the apparent safety of the warren is in fact a human trap where death lies carefully hidden.

The sense of an unseen menace haunts *Watership Down* as it does Adams's other works of fiction. In *Watership Down* it is the dark shadow of the humans, who remain largely invisible but whose works – the car, the snare, the lethal gas, the 'white blindness' of myxomatosis –

produce a level of fear beyond that of even the stoat and the fox.

That fear is tangible because Adams takes the reader inside the rabbits' existence. He famously relied on R. M. Lockley's book *The Private Life of the Rabbit* to flesh out his own observations, but he was clearly fascinated by rabbits' fugitive lives and the ground-level world they inhabit. Fiver, Hazel, Bigwig, Dandelion and the others embody the realities of the natural world and the subtle understanding of it that is not open to humans: 'the passing of time is something that civilized human beings have lost the power to feel. Creatures that have neither clocks nor books are alive to all manner of knowledge . . .'

A strong sense of the natural world and its potential fragility runs through *Watership Down*. The rabbits are threatened by both humans and their natural predators. By the time they reach Watership Down after many days and nights of travelling they are feeling the strain of prolonged insecurity and fear. And their eventual arrival proves something of a false dawn.

The continued existence of the new warren depends on the presence of females, so the rabbits organize an expedition to capture some does from another warren that lies even further to the south. Leading it is the despotic General Woundwort. The final third of the book describes the rabbits' infiltration of Woundwort's brutal regime, the capture of the does and the General's relentless pursuit of them back to Watership Down where a final, bloody confrontation takes place. The account of the trickery involved in this enterprise and of the long battle with General Woundwort and his violent lieutenants is a terrific piece of storytelling in which bravery, determination and guile triumph over brute strength and superior resources.

But it's in Adams's evocation of the beauty, complexity and 'otherness' of nature that the magic of *Watership Down* lies. Here is his description of the rabbits' first sight of the down in the last of the evening sun:

The light, full and smooth, lay like a gold rind over the turf.

> But down in the grass itself, between the bushes, in that thick forest trodden by the beetle, the spider and the hunting shrew, the light was like a wind that danced among them to set them scurrying and weaving. The red rays flickered in and out of the grass stems, flashing minutely on membranous wings . . .

Adams was clearly in love with the place and possessed the knowledge of the tiny details of nature and landscape that comes from close observation, and it was clearly a place he wanted to share with his readers. Perhaps that is why he didn't give fictional names to any of the farms, brooks, heaths, downs or copses.

And just like Richard Adams, Fiver, Hazel, Bigwig and the others, we've been beguiled by the down and the surrounding landscape. I now know the fields where the stone curlews that arrive from the Mediterranean each spring come to nest. But I've also come to know the land's features in relation to where Bigwig met the fox or where Woundwort rallied his troops.

Watership Down is much more than just a children's book or a morality tale because it has come to mean so much to so many people. I revel in friends' reactions when we take them up to see the down. It's as if I've just pointed out Egdon Heath, the Hundred Acre Wood or Barchester Cathedral. One day the book's popularity may be the down's saving grace, for with it Richard Adams has created a generation of readers who will surely act as conservationists for this unique place.

COLIN WILLIAMS is a writer on nature, landscape and human heritage. Raised among the birds, sky and water of the Norfolk fens he now lives and writes on Hampshire's chalk downlands.

The illustration at the beginning of this article is reproduced courtesy of the Estate of Robert Gibbings and the Heather Chalcroft Literary Agency.

Inspired by Kipling

DAVID GILMOUR

When recently I began to write a social history of British India, I realized I would have to keep Rudyard Kipling under control. I could not endlessly compare people to characters in a Kipling story or make points and then back them up with 'As Kipling once wrote . . .' Nor could I write about scandals in Simla and describe them as Kiplingesque scenarios.

I hadn't realized, however, that I would also have to exercise control over Kipling's place in the minds of many of the people I was writing about. Yet from the 1880s onwards he appears as a regular influence, from schooldays to career choice, to work and leisure, and even to retirement. When writing his memoirs, one figure of the Indian Civil Service (ICS) could not resist beginning a sentence with 'If, as Kipling says (always Kipling) . . .' Here I shall be writing about how Kipling inspired people to go to India and how they looked at it through his eyes; a subsequent article will examine how those same people lived their lives with Kipling at their shoulder (as it were), and how accurate they considered his portrait of British India might be.

Born in Bombay on the penultimate day of 1865, young 'Ruddy' spent five and a half years in India before he was taken to England with his younger sister Trix and left there for eleven years of school-

---

Rudyard Kipling, *Plain Tales from the Hills* (1888) · Penguin · Pb · 336pp · £8.99 · ISBN 9780141442396; *Kim* (1901) · Penguin · Pb · 432pp · £8.99 · ISBN 9780141442372.

Departmental Ditties (1886), *Under the Deodars* (1888) and *Barrack-Room Ballads* (1892) are available as print-on-demand books or second-hand.

Donald Maxwell, 'The Gateway of India', from Kipling's *East of Suez*

ing. In 1882 he returned to the country of his birth to work as a journalist on the *Civil and Military Gazette* in Lahore, where his father was curator of the museum and principal of the Mayo School of Industrial Arts. Displaying a precocity that astonished and sometimes exasperated his contemporaries, he had his first book of poems (*Departmental Ditties and Other Verses*) published in 1886 when he was 20, and his first collection of stories (*Plain Tales from the Hills*) two years later. Many other stories of India (and a few further poems) were to come, some published while he was still living in Lahore, others when he moved to Allahabad in 1887, and more after he had left India in 1889. 'Gunga Din', 'Danny Deever' and 'Mandalay' were written in 1890 and published as part of *Barrack-Room Ballads* in 1892. *Kim*, that magical picaresque novel, did not appear until 1901.

Kipling's verse and fiction became popular very quickly in British India. People started giving his books as presents, often accompanied by notes observing that their contents were 'so true to life': as late as the 1930s one ICS officer sent his fiancée in England the complete works 'to prepare' her for what was to come. Kipling's verse, its strong rhythms making it easy to remember, became a useful weapon for the bore. 'Bobby lay on his back and recited yards and yards of Kipling,' is one memsahib's diary record of a picnic near Mhow. 'You're a better man than I am, Gunga Din' became a favourite line for men who wanted others to know that they appreciated the good qualities of Indians. Even today, when people hear I have written about Kipling, I see them struggling with memory before coming out with lines such as 'If you can meet with Triumph and Disaster/And treat those two impostors just the same . . .'

Once his books were circulating in Britain, Kipling acted as an unofficial, and indeed unwitting, recruiting agent for three generations of British boys who were inspired by him to go to India.

Philip Mason, a distinguished civil servant and a writer in retirement, was one of them. When in old age he was asked why he had joined the ICS, he replied with one word, 'Kipling'. Not only had the stories, which as a child he had known almost by heart, given him a 'romantic desire' to go to India; 'with their strong sense of commitment to duties usually unpleasant and often dangerous', they had inspired him to go and carry out those duties himself. When eventually he got to the northern plains, as he recalled in his memoir, *A Shaft of Sunlight*, he 'became aware of a sensation almost of coming home'; he was remembering 'the scents of dust and spices' from his reading of Kipling. It was these, together with the thought of 'the bright colours of the bazaar', that had drawn him to India in the first place. I have similar feelings even now when I am in Mumbai and visit the Crawford Markets (their entrance decorated with beautiful bas-reliefs designed by Kipling's father).

Although the ICS was appreciated as a service that was efficient, just and incorruptible, Kipling himself was not an unqualified admirer; his fictional portraits of civil servants are sometimes less than flattering. Yet his work evidently had a special resonance with candidates for the ICS. One of them recalled how Kipling had 'cast his spell' through his prep-school headmaster's readings from *Kim*, and 'the magic persisted'. Another had no Indian connections and was reluctantly planning to follow his father into the family flour mill when he read Kipling and was inspired to take the ICS exam at

Burlington House in Piccadilly. When Herbert Thompson went out in 1922 as a civil servant to Madras (which Kipling had neither visited nor written about), he admitted that his 'only general source of information about India lay in the works of Rudyard Kipling', all of whose books he had read. His ICS contemporary Maurice Zinkin was in an even more advanced state of ignorance, confessing that no one in his family had ever been east of Suez and that his own knowledge of India was confined to *Kim* and *The Jungle Book*. In this he was matched by his future wife, a French girl called Tanya. As a child she had memorized *The Jungle Book* in her own language, reading and rereading the story of Mowgli and the death of Akela without ever realizing that 'Kipling was not French like Jules Verne . . .'

Reading such memories often makes me regret that I never read Kipling as a child (his books were not on our nursery shelves because my father's collection had been appropriated by my aunt). I discovered Kipling as an adult. So did Arthur Hamilton, who had been wounded in the First World War, and was mesmerized when he read Kipling in convalescence: once demobbed, he applied to the India Office, studied forestry at Oxford and went out to the Punjab as an official of the Forest Department. Yet Kipling's appeal was not limited just to men eager to join the army or one of the services.

Whatever racial assumptions and imperialist feelings he may have had – and which he shared with most of his generation – Kipling's love of India was unquestionable, and he communicated it in a way that was accessible to all. His impact on Ernest Hartley was such that in 1905 the 22-year-old abandoned his middle-class life in Yorkshire for a job as a junior exchange broker in a firm in Calcutta. He did not achieve any great things there, and his name might not have survived in print had he not become the father of the actress Vivien Leigh, who shared his love of Kipling.

Youthful admirers in England were seldom disappointed when they reached Kipling's India. One engineer found that at the Victoria Terminus in Bombay 'the platform was all that Kipling described and

A drawing by Norah Vivian, the wife of an ICS officer, 1930s

[he] felt like looking round for Kim among the crowd of passengers'. Others felt the presence of the young imp with his lama on the Grand Trunk Road or up among the deodars at Simla, where Mason identified 'the place where Kim met Lurgan Sahib', or even further up amid the snows of the Himalayas. The writer John Masters recognized those mountains because he 'had travelled in them too, with

Kim'. It was in the pages of *Kim*, 'the best book . . . ever written on India', that Masters first had 'felt the tang of the air and heard the silence, and seen [with Kim] "the appalling sweep and dispersal of the cloud shadows after rain"'.

Masters also recognized the Seeonee Hills, the location of the Jungle Books, as did an ICS officer, Noël Tindal Porter, for whom service there was 'the realization of a dream', because he had been brought up on those books. Masters rhapsodized about 'Kipling's genius for transmitting atmosphere', but the genius in this case was even greater than he realized, because Kipling had never in fact visited the Seeonee.

As an adult Kipling lived in India for only six and a half years and spent most of his time in Lahore in the Punjab. Many of his devotees were naturally sent to other parts of India and were correspondingly disappointed with what they found. Vivien Stevenson-Hamilton, a subaltern in the 4th Gurkhas, was frustrated at his posting to the North-West Frontier because it was far away from anywhere described in *Kim* and the *Plain Tales*; fortunately he was soon able to wangle a transfer into the heart of Kipling country as an ADC to the governor of the Punjab, based in Lahore in the cold weather and in Simla in summer.

Another subaltern in the Indian Army, H. R. Robinson, was even more desperate. Hoping to experience the 'colourful glamour of the East', he was understandably dismayed by his initial train journey from Karachi – 'a vista of desert and barren hills, sweltering heat and very little shade' – and then so depressed by Baluchistan that his 'soul thirsted' for something else. He looked at the map, identified the Bay of Bengal and recalled the 'cleaner, greener land' of Kipling's 'Mandalay'. So he got himself transferred to Burma, was seduced by the charm of the country and its people, and became in turn a policeman, a frontier official and a Buddhist mendicant. Unfortunately he also became an opium addict and spent all the money he had – and some he did not have – on his addiction. On being arrested for trying to abscond without paying his debts, he grabbed his pistol and tried to kill himself while reciting Kipling's lines from 'The Young British Soldier':

> When you're wounded and left on Afghanistan's plains,
> And the women come out to cut up what remains,
> Jest roll to your rifle and blow out your brains
> An' go to your Gawd like a soldier.

The attempt only blinded him, but it did cure his addiction.

Kipling spent a mere three days in Burma, at the end of his years in India, yet he managed to evoke the country in a handful of nouns and half a dozen verses in 'Mandalay'.

> For the wind is in the palm-trees, and the temple-bells they say:
> 'Come you back, you British soldier; come you back to
> Mandalay!'

Kipling knew the British soldier ('Tommy Atkins') and he knew the life of the bazaars as no other British writer has ever known them. So he would not have been surprised to learn that for years afterwards Burmese girls of the oldest profession would try to entice Tommies into their beds with the line, 'Come you back, you British soldier . . .' But as an imperialist sceptical of the merits of democracy, he would certainly have been surprised to learn that his poem came to be so revered by a Burmese democratic leader, Aung San Suu Kyi, that an extract was read out at her wedding.

She also had an unusual view of Kipling's 'If', a poem whose detractors and supporters generally line up on either side of the Left/Right divide. Chile's communist poet, Pablo Neruda, dismissed it as 'that uninspired, sanctimonious . . . precursor of *Reader's Digest*, whose intellectual level . . . was no higher than the Duke of Alba's shoes'. (He had found a framed copy of the poem in Gothic lettering by the duke's bedside in the Madrid palace abandoned by the family in the Spanish Civil War.) Aung San Suu Kyi disagreed. The work, she observed, may often have been 'dismissed as the epitome of imperial bombast', but it was in fact 'a great poem for dissidents'. She even produced a Burmese translation to inspire her supporters.

Aung San Suu Kyi is not the most improbable admirer of Kipling. When reviewing T. S. Eliot's introduction to Kipling's verse in 1942, George Orwell began a tradition in which left-wing and anti-colonialist writers praised Kipling's work while damning his politics and sometimes his character. Two prominent members of this group have been Edward Said and Salman Rushdie. When asked by Penguin to introduce two collections of early stories, *Soldiers Three* and *In Black and White*, Rushdie accepted the invitation and concluded his essay with the words, 'There will always be plenty in Kipling that I will find difficult to forgive; but there is also enough truth in these stories to make them impossible to ignore.'

The sequel to this article will appear in Issue 55.

DAVID GILMOUR is the author of *The Long Recessional*, a life of Kipling, who also makes guest appearances in his *Curzon* and *The Ruling Caste*. But the author has managed to exclude him from his Italian books.

Keeping It Real

MAGGIE FERGUSSON

The undergraduates have yet to return for the next academic term, and Cambridge is asleep. On the sunny ten-minute walk from the station to Ali Smith's house I pass barely a soul. So it's good that Ali has emailed clear instructions. 'Turn right up a tiny road,' they conclude. 'It looks like a driveway. It's our street.' In fact, when you reach it, it feels neither like a driveway nor a street, but more like a small enchanted world – a terrace of little cottages on one side, tiny gardens opposite. Ali and her partner, Sarah, live in one of the cottages and work in another, and it's in the working one that Ali's waiting for me, in a room full of towers of books and old LPs. I sink into a low sofa, and across the rush mat opposite me Ali, small, dark and bright-eyed, settles cross-legged on a large cushion. Her black and white cat weaves to and fro between us.

As a child growing up in a council house in the Scottish Highlands, Ali says, she was 'shy and outgoing – both at once', and perhaps this is true of her still. Reading her books, and meeting her in person, you can't but feel warmed by her generosity, her bursting desire to share her enthusiasms and insights, and her appetite for life. But at the same time she's ambivalent about the public personae writers these days are obliged to adopt. 'You have to develop a means of surviving it,' she says, 'and either that becomes a performative self or for me

---

Ali Smith's *Hotel World* (2001), *The Accidental* (2005) and *How to Be Both* (2014) are all available as paperbacks from Penguin, at £8.99 each. Her latest novel, *Autumn* (2016), is available in hardback from Hamish Hamilton (272pp · £16.99 · ISBN 9780241207000).

it's meant devising a self who can still be the real self talking about real things, like I am now to you.' Speaking on stage at festivals is exhausting, she says, and she doesn't really enjoy it. 'But I've developed a means of dealing with it. I used to just get angry. I've trained myself to stop being annoyed that I've got to be in public.'

It's fifteen years since Ali's second novel, *Hotel World*, won the Encore Award and was shortlisted for both the Orange Prize and the Man Booker, propelling her into the limelight. Four years later, in 2005, *The Accidental* was shortlisted for both those prizes again and won the Whitbread Novel of the Year Award. Then in 2014 *How to Be Both* swept the board – shortlisted for the Booker and winning the Baileys Women's Prize for Fiction, the Folio Prize, the Goldsmiths Prize and the Costa Novel Award. It's a joyful, energetic, deeply moving novel which plaits together the stories of a Renaissance painter, Francesco del Cossa, and a twenty-first-century Cambridge schoolgirl, George, and it's a very hard act to follow. But, when we meet, Ali is riding high on the critical success of a new novel, *Autumn*. At its heart is the friendship between Elisabeth, an 11-year-old whom we follow into adulthood, and her wise and wonderful next-door neighbour, Daniel, who lives to be over 100. It's both playful and deadly serious, and bubbling through it are the stories of Christine Keeler, the Pop artist Pauline Boty and Brexit.

'I'd been writing since the beginning of last year,' she says, 'and already the book was about how you cross divisions, how you cross seas into other countries, how you exist as a being with an identity in a world becoming ever more bordered.' Then in May she began to suspect that the vote would go for Brexit, and 'in June I realized it was getting very close . . . And then suddenly it had happened!' She snaps her fingers. The book was to have been delivered in late June, but she asked her editor, Simon Prosser at Hamish Hamilton, to give her an extra month 'to allow what had happened to percolate'. This may not have been comfortable in terms of publishing schedules – most novelists have deadlines a year ahead of publication and *Autumn* was due out in October – but it enabled her to produce what Prosser describes as 'the most contemporaneous novel I've ever read'. She spent the rest of the year promoting it, as well as 'doing some library stuff' (she is a passionate defender of public libraries, and is appalled by the numbers closing). Then in January she battened down the hatches to get started on *Winter*, the second in her four-book seasonal cycle.

Does she research hard before starting, I wonder? By way of a reply she tells me about a dinner party some years back at which she was seated next to Tom Stoppard.

> I told him I'd been in *The Real Inspector Hound* when I was 14, and he told me that he was working on a piece about the early work of Pink Floyd. So I said, 'Are you going back into the archives to research stuff?' And he stopped me and said, 'No! Never do that! Whatever you are doing *never* go so far into it that the imagination is lost. If there's a piece of evidence from a time, say it's a letter, don't go back and read the letter, just lift the envelope a bit and peek in, otherwise you'll just reproduce the letter, and what's the point of that?' In other words, allow your imagination to work with what comes at you tangentially. What a wise person!

Ali believes in serendipity. Like Virginia Woolf in *The Common Reader*, she feels that the best way to read is randomly – 'just to pick up a book off a pile', and then to allow it to spark connections. And when she's not reading but is out and about in the world she tunes into what people are saying around her, and how they are saying it. As readers of her novels will know, she is intrigued by officialese.

> Back in 1995 I went up to Hebden Bridge to do an Arvon guest appearance, and in the middle of the night we'd all gone down to look at Sylvia Plath's grave. It was a frosty night; we walked down with torches. Next morning I got on the train, and I had

a piece of stick with me that I'd picked up near Plath's grave. In one carriage of the train everybody was speaking a language that I hadn't realized was being spoken which was businessese. And I stood with my stick knowing I was from another time. It was a realization of the Kafkaesque, of the absurdities in the ways we use language to create systems. I'm fascinated by that.

The front door is open as we chat, and outside a white van has drawn up with 'Paul Bailey Flooring' emblazoned on its side. Ali has a good laugh imagining her dear friend Paul Bailey the novelist and critic in a new incarnation as a carpet-layer, before we move on to talk about her childhood.

She was born in 1962, the youngest of five children, to parents who had, through poverty, been forced to leave school at 13. 'Both my parents were fiercely intelligent,' she says; both had scholarships that they weren't able to take up. At 14 her mother became a conductor on buses travelling up and down the coast of the Moray Firth, while her father became an electrician. Ali remembers his shop as an Aladdin's cave where he could always find exactly what was needed. He was honest and good-humoured – both qualities he has passed on to his youngest daughter. 'When I was very small we went to visit a dying neighbour,' Ali says. 'He was sitting in the front room and everyone around him was like this' – she pulls a long face – 'and my father said, "What's this Andy, not dead yet?" and the whole place erupted with laughter, most of all the dying man. And I realized then my father's power to say the thing that had to be said: to make things better and to be truthful at the same time.'

Her mother, meantime, was 'very proper and very mischievous', both at once. Saturday night was bath night – 'the immersion heater went on and we had our baths before church on Sunday' – and after her bath her mother would sit her on her knee and become different characters. 'She would just drop out of herself, I mean as if in a trance, and it was terrifying, absolutely terrifying.'

Ali was seven years younger than the next sibling up – so 'there were four kids ahead of me. They certainly gave me a hard time, but they also protected me absolutely. It was a very stable and lovely way to grow up. It meant I could inhabit my own world and at the same time know about all sorts of other worlds and be part of them.' Family lore has it that when she was 3 Ali taught herself to read by scrutinizing the labels on her siblings' records. 'I'm presuming there's some truth in it. What I do remember is the first time I recognized the word "exactly". I clearly remember seeing the word and realizing it was the word "exactly", and the lightning point of marrying up a word with its written version, and the charge of energy you get when that happens.'

After their Saturday-evening baths, Sunday morning meant church for all the family. Ali's mother was a devout Catholic and had persuaded her father ('God knows how') to convert. When it came to the sermon, Ali developed a way of going to sleep with her eyes open, allowing her mind to wander. Yet although she has long since stopped going to church, she's not sure that she's given up Catholicism – 'I'm not sure that you *can* give it up. And it's given me this gift: the gift of the reality of metaphor. You cannot avoid the reality of transubstantiation. So it's given me that particular present – the present of the present as it were: a moment at which something can be itself and yet be something else.' Meantime she's now moved and impressed by Pope Francis. 'Truly, if I think of the statespeople at large in the world today going out of their way to make the world better rather than to make it more cordoned off and money-producing for the very rich, I think of Nicola Sturgeon and Pope Francis! They're, I don't know, *echt*, the real thing.'

Both of Ali's parents were determined that all five children should go to university, so from school Ali went on to Aberdeen, then to Cambridge to do a Ph.D., then back north to a lecturing job at Strathclyde. It was 1991 and 'the universities were flooded with students so that there weren't enough seats, and students – whom we were told to call clients – had to sit outside and watch lectures by video link-up. I'd come through a system which had been one-to-one, and the seminars were now forty people and the tutorials twenty people, and the notion that I couldn't remember the names of the people I was teaching – well, I found it a very unhappy experience.' In the midst of all this her mother died, and Ali was knocked sideways – 'we live in a society that doesn't prepare us for grief, or for the whirligig of time'. Diagnosed with Chronic Fatigue Syndrome, she moved back to Cambridge and started tentatively to write stories – partly in order to get her hands and arms to work again. Her first collection, *Free Love and Other Stories*, was published in 1995, and won the Saltire First Book Award. She was launched.

Outside Paul Bailey is packing up his van when his mobile goes off. The ring tone is the theme tune from *Steptoe and Son*, and Ali creases up with laughter again. I have a last question: has writing got harder or easier? Does she relish or fear the blank page? 'You don't get a choice,' she replies without hesitation. 'For me, anyway, the first line just appears. And then you're off.'

MAGGIE FERGUSSON is Literary Director of the Royal Society of Literature and has written biographies of George Mackay Brown and Michael Morpurgo.

Speaking Volumes

CONSTANTINE FRASER

When a people disappears, they say the last thing to be forgotten is its food. You might not teach your children your mother tongue, but the chances are you'll still cook them your mother's recipes.

Thessaloniki today seems a thoroughly Greek place – all Byzantine churches and pork skewers. But at the turn of the twentieth century the Ottoman port then called Salonika was a very different city. Half its inhabitants were Sephardic Jews, who had arrived in the area after their expulsion from Spain in 1492. They still named their synagogues after their lost Iberian homeland – Aragon, Catalan – and they spoke Ladino, a Hebrew-inflected dialect of medieval Spanish. The rest of the townsfolk were a mix of Turkish-speaking Muslims and Greek and Bulgarian Christians who lived in different districts and worked in different trades. So long as all obeyed the Sultan's laws and paid his taxes, the empire's authorities did not care whether their subjects shared Ottoman values or were culturally integrated. Salonika was multicultural *avant la lettre*.

In the opening pages of *Salonika: A Family Cookbook*, by Esin Eden and Nicholas Stavroulakis, the latter calls the old city

> an ancient house with many rooms, shared by different families whose paths only crossed in darkened corridors . . . Some rooms were full of light and open to the changes that were

---

Esin Eden and Nicholas Stavroulakis, *Salonika: A Family Cookbook* (1997), is published by Talos Press, Athens. Copies can be ordered through the Etz Hayyim synagogue in Chania: contact info@etz-hayyim-hania.org.

taking place in the world about this house, but others were dark, cradling hidden memories and events that were seldom, if ever, brought to light.

Now, the reader might raise a sceptical eyebrow at the words 'family cookbook'. Personally, they make me think of spinsterly great-aunts with a taste for self-publishing. This is no jam-making memoir, however: it's a last culinary record of a lost culture, and a window into a dark, tightly shuttered room. Esin Eden is a well-known Turkish actress, and her family – whose recipes these are – were members of Salonika's strangest and most secretive sect. They called themselves Ma'aminim or Believers; to the rest of the world they were Dönme, the Turkish for 'turncoats'.

The Dönme were the Salonika-based followers of a seventeenth-century rabbi and self-proclaimed Messiah, Sabbatai Zevi. In the autumn of 1666, threatened by the Sultan with impalement, Sabbatai purchased his life by publicly converting to Islam. Thousands of his devotees interpreted this as a test of their faith and followed him into apostasy, but they continued to observe Jewish customs behind closed doors, mixing elements of Sufism and the Kabbalah with Sabbatai's own mystical teachings. Each individual had two names: a Turkish name used in the outside world, and a Hebrew name revealed only to intimate acquaintances. According to the historian Gershom Scholem, there even exists strong evidence that – among their various ecstatic rites – the Dönme practised ritual wife-swapping.

Though untraditional in more ways than one, they also had the city's best schools, and by the turn of the twentieth century the 10,000 Dönme were one of the most highly educated and secular of Salonika's communities. Photographs of Eden's relatives show sensitive men in tall starched collars engrossed in the latest European fiction – Wildean dandies with olive skin and improbable moustaches. Dönme women were also some of the most liberated in the empire. In Eden's family, 'all of them were fluent in French, German and, of course, Osmanli [Ottoman Turkish], and the latest editions of novels and poetry were always appearing in the house'.

As for Nicholas Stavroulakis, Eden's co-author and illustrator, a photograph on the back cover shows him half-shrouded in darkness, his one visible eyebrow raised at the camera. An artist, a scholar and a founder of Greece's Jewish Museum, he has rescued a Cretan synagogue from ruin, and there in advanced old age he presides over a congregation which numbers as many gentiles – drawn there out of sheer affection for him – as it does Jews. His life's work has been to keep alive the memory of Greece's cosmopolitan past, and he lurks in the acknowledgements pages of every book to have been published on Salonika or on Ottoman Jewry over the past few decades. The author photograph has him at his desk, a sort of rabbinic monk-scribe – his task to remember, to record and to illuminate.

Some of the Dönme recipes look Greek: moussaka, stuffed vine leaves and egg-and-lemon sauces. Clearly Turkish are the *kapama* meats steamed with onion under lettuce leaves, and rice pilafs named after officers of the Janissary corps. I started by having a stab at an old Sephardic starter, *huevos en haminados* – hard-boiled eggs, simmered for hour after hour with onion skins, coffee grounds and used tea leaves until they're stained a deep brown. They looked intriguingly pointless. The result: nutty, slightly fleshier-than-normal hard-boiled eggs. Perfectly nice, but nothing to write home about. Other Salonikan Jewish classics include fish in walnut sauce, and meatballs stewed in sweet green plums with the appealing name of *bobotas*.

But the cookbook isn't just a collation of Greek, Turkish and Sephardic dishes. Dönme cuisine also gives a direct insight into religious practices kept so tightly under wraps that it was not until the 1930s that one of their miniaturized, handwritten prayer books fell into an outsider's hands. Sabbatai Zevi had instructed his followers to observe all the rituals of Islam, so there are kebabs for after sunset during Ramadan and mourning sweets for Ashura, which commemorates the deaths of Mohammed's grandsons Hasan and Husayn.

Nicholas Stavroulakis (from his *Cookbook of the Jews of Greece*, Lycabettus Press)

Ashura was particularly important to the Dönme, for whom Sabbatai was the latest incarnation of the divine spirit that Shi'a Muslims also claim passed down from Mohammed to his successors.

Many of the Sephardic recipes have been modified to cook meat with butter, in defiance of Jewish dietary laws. Sabbatai claimed that his anointment as Messiah ushered in a new age, in which the written law of the Torah was revoked and what was forbidden became obligatory – hence also his followers' unorthodox sexual behaviour. But cooking meat with dairy is also a clear Turkish influence: Jews are traditionally forbidden from mixing the two, and Greek Christians rarely cook in anything but olive oil. Just as the Dönme had to turn Turk, so did their Sephardic cuisine.

Not much is left of old Salonika or the Dönme. Greece annexed Salonika in 1912. Under the terms of the Treaty of Lausanne in 1923, the country expelled its Muslims in exchange for Turkey's Orthodox Christians, and the Dönme were shipped off with them – notwithstanding their protestations that they were not true Muslims. Mostly settling in Istanbul, they quickly became a favourite subject for conspiracy theorists, and fear and isolation drove them to assimilate into mainstream Turkish society. Meanwhile, back in Salonika – by now renamed Thessaloniki – the Holocaust would be the final step in the city's becoming homogeneously Greek. When Esin Eden travelled for the first time to her parents' home,

> the old great houses had been torn down and the gardens destroyed. Gone were the huge walnut trees that provided the nuts for fish recipes and Nuriye's sweets all through the year . . . It was all gone.

On the Asian side of Istanbul, however, in the cemetery at Bülbülderesi – the Valley of the Nightingales – there are gravestones decorated with photographs of smartly dressed, sensitive-looking Turks, and with delicate carvings of butterflies. Their descendants, presumably, still live in the city. If any are reading this, do get in touch.

CONSTANTINE FRASER is a postgraduate at the LSE. He spends much of his spare time conducting research into Eastern Mediterranean cuisine.

Everyday Mysteries

MICHAEL HOLROYD

In the autumn of 2008, in issue no. 19, *Slightly Foxed* published an essay by Richard Ingrams. He had chosen John Stewart Collis's book called *The Worm Forgives the Plough* – a title taken from William Blake's 'Proverbs of Hell'. The book had been written (originally in two volumes with different titles) during the Second World War when Collis, then in his forties, had become one of the agricultural labourers who took the place of farmworkers conscripted by the army. This was an inspiring period of his career during which he produced his literary classic – a judgement that was endorsed when in 2009 Vintage added the book to its list of classics with a compelling introduction by Robert Macfarlane.

'To work as a labourer on the land had been a great desire of mine,' Collis wrote. This was his adult education. He learnt harrowing and ditching, ploughing and haymaking and harvesting – and finally he cleared the wild entanglement of an ash wood later to be named 'Collis Piece'. Occasionally he would revisit this wood.

Title-page decoration by Barbara Allen for John Stewart Collis's *The Worm Forgives the Plough*

John Stewart Collis, *Shaw* (1925), *An Irishman's England* (1937), *Marriage and Genius: Strindberg and Tolstoy* (1963), *Leo Tolstoy* (1969), *The Carlyles* (1971), *Bound upon a Course* (1971) and *Christopher Columbus* (1976) are all out of print, but we can obtain second-hand copies.

'Nobody is ever likely to confer upon me Honours or Titles or city freedoms, nor will any Monument be raised to perpetuate and repeat my name,' he wrote. 'But this plot of earth will do it, these trees will do it: in the summer they will glitter and shine for me, and in the winter, mourn.'

The danger of being known as the author of a single masterpiece is that your other books may unjustly be neglected. Certainly Collis's biographies and autobiographies, his ecology and fiction are too original to be forgotten.

He was born in Killiney to the south of Dublin where his father worked as a solicitor. He was a younger twin, their mother giving all her love to the elder one. 'From the hour of my birth she hated me,' he wrote. 'Ours was not a united family.' To escape from such unhappiness his father sent him to England for his education: to Rugby, then to Balliol College, Oxford, to which he claimed to have gained entrance by some judicious cheating in Latin Unseen. 'I hankered after oratory,' he wrote, and he practised public speaking in debates with G. K. Chesterton, W. B. Yeats and other visiting writers.

While still a schoolboy Collis had seen Bernard Shaw's political comedy *John Bull's Other Island* at the Abbey Theatre in Dublin. 'It was like hearing heavenly music – and I knew that at last I was feeling the real thing.' His first publication, 'a new book on an old subject', written in his early twenties, was simply called *Shaw.* Collis explains in his one-paragraph preface that

> some books are written for the pleasure of the reader and the profit of the writer, some for the profit of the reader and the pleasure of the writer, and some simply insist upon being written in spite of reader and writer . . . [They] are often a great nuisance to the writer as well as to everybody else, but nevertheless they must be written. This is such a book.

There is a sense of necessity in the writing which Shaw could not help liking. Most biographers who wrote about GBS during his lifetime had their pens taken from them while he rewrote many of their pages. But when Collis gave his chapters to Shaw, he replied with letters parts of which he allowed Collis to use as footnotes. They cover all sorts of subjects from vegetarian diets 'for poets and philosophers' to critics of Shakespeare from Voltaire to Dr Johnson (both quite different from Shaw's own criticism of Victorian bardolators such as Henry Irving). One footnote is a single word: 'Hooray!' (It would make an amusing test to ask Shavian scholars what they thought Collis could have written to bring forth such a cheer. The sentence was: 'I fancy he has gained far more from listening to Wagner and Mozart than he has gained from all his reading put together.')

The Shaw who emerges from Collis's book is a man who conceals his generosity and is more often praised than understood by the public. He makes plenty of mistakes but often learns from them and is a believer in evolution rather than revolution. The book was published in 1925 and was reprinted three times, gaining Collis some money to which he added £150 by selling his letters from Shaw. With this he soon set off abroad.

'Etna's volcano being in eruption I decided to go to Sicily at once and climb the mountain up to the crater if possible,' he later wrote in his autobiography, *Bound upon a Course* (1971). This book has its strengths and its limitations. There were gaps in his own life which were too painful to revisit at any length – in particular his unhappy childhood and unfortunate first marriage.

He had married an American girl whom he had known for just one week. She believed he was a genius and would make a fortune. But he never did and she eventually decided he was a total failure. Meanwhile she became a medical pioneer with an intuitional flair for helping children with cerebral palsy. In the 1950s she herself was struck down with cerebral thrombosis. For six years Collis looked after her day and night – then for another six years she went into a nursing home – and one night she suddenly died. 'She had been dying slowly before my eyes for years,' he wrote. 'My friends thought it would be a release for me as well as for her . . . I did not know my own heart. I did not know when the time came I would not be able to bear her *non-existence.*'

His marriage led him to study other people's marriages and produce a new category of Life Writing. 'Few of us know much about the married life even of our closest friends,' he wrote. 'Nothing is guarded so secretly as this matter. We do know something about the marriages of the famous whose lives have been documented by themselves and others. I have often thought that it is the same story as that of undocumented millions; the same story writ large.'

His three dual biographies cover the multiplicity of Strindberg's wives, the complexity of Tolstoy's marriage to Sonya and the charming courtship and discordant later life of Thomas and Jane Welsh Carlyle. The originality of these tight, swiftly moving narratives with their ever-increasing drama did not depend upon unpublished documents. He read all the published correspondence, biographies and diaries he could find. Then he reinterpreted what he had read. A good example of his ability to merge comedy with tragedy comes from his reading of Aylmer Maude's book *The Final Struggle* with its last photograph of Tolstoy with his wife. It made an extraordinary impact on Collis. This is what he wrote:

> September 23rd was the anniversary of their wedding. She was determined that a photograph should be taken of them together as a loving couple. He tried to get out of it, feeling embarrassed and ashamed. But she overruled all objections, and the photograph was taken . . . She was determined to make him turn his face towards her and smile. But he would not. He had often and often been deliberately gentle, with a loving word, or by giving her a pear, or by saying how pleased he was to see her eating pancakes – all duly noted in her diary. But not now. Here was a test (we never quite know when we are being tested)

> of the depth of his Christianity and the absoluteness of his cheek-turning principles. It would have been easy to have looked in her direction and given her a smile. He would not . . . He looked to the front as hard as a cliff, and as obstinate. And there she stands, in her frightful clothes and her fierce possessive regard, and with a couple of handcuffs she has clapped upon him. And there he stands in the coarse blouse and the leather belt that he always wore . . . a blind but unconquered Samson.

Despite his engaging life of Christopher Columbus (1976), Collis was not a talented traveller. His adventurous journeys were often less dramatic than the strolls he made round London and described in *An Irishman's England* (1937). Earlier, when wearing gym shoes and carrying his satchel, he had climbed to the very edge of Etna's erupting crater, he saw nothing except clouds of sulphurous smoke. But travelling at rush hour by Tube across London he fell – not to the ground but into a crowd of passengers that, as they swept along, held him at an angle of forty-five degrees. 'I have often wondered at the endurance of the people hanging up there on their straps like dead animals . . . they all insist upon coming home at the same moment, and hundreds who could go back by boat along the Thames in summer refuse to do so.' There was, he concluded, 'too little despair in this city . . . Therefore not enough hope. Only endurance.' The secret of London, he concluded, was the secret of beauty itself which arises, like Love and Truth, 'out of the agony of the world'. It is not surprising that Robert Macfarlane believed that Collis belonged to the same literary family as another Irish writer, Samuel Beckett.

There is the orator's voice in much of Collis's writing. His description of travelling to Rotherhithe to buy a chair has something of Beckett's humour of desolation. After a good deal of waiting, the journey began.

> We arrived at Stepney – but not at our destination. We got into

> a bus: we got out of it. We got into a tram and out of it. We crossed streets and changed into more trams. We stood in the wind . . . It was a cold and bloodless day, and at that hour of the afternoon when all meaning is withdrawn from the universe. And in the midst, our guide . . . a timeless expression on her face. She was coming to help us buy this chair . . . she stood in the tram, waited by the kerb, walked through the alleys – wholly indifferent to the world . . . Her figure assumed a gigantic shape . . . the atlas of injustice.

An Irishman's England is dotted with short sentences as he reflects on diverse aspects of England between the two world wars. 'I once met a man walking up Charing Cross Road,' he wrote, 'accompanied by a small elephant.' Yet no one else seems to notice this. One windy day he takes cover and sees a birdlike woman blown 'in all the plumes of her sophistication, from Upper to Lower Regent Street'. He describes Marble Arch as 'a gateway leading nowhere' – perhaps a metaphor for the whole country.

In some fifteen books Collis focused on the 'extraordinary nature of the ordinary'. He was essentially a poet who studied the sciences, discovering the mysteries of what we take for granted. 'He was *sui generis*,' wrote A. N. Wilson who as literary editor of the *Spectator* was 'happy to publish anything he wrote' towards the end of Collis's life. 'He survives in his books,' Wilson adds. But what would bring him alive for a new generation of readers would be an anthology of the best pages from these neglected publications.

MICHAEL HOLROYD is currently writing a play and co-editing a volume of letters in the hope of producing as many dissimilar publications as John Stewart Collis.

Stranger in Paradise

JOHN KEAY

The beauty of short books is that you can afford to read them more than once. In the case of Nicolas Bouvier's *The Scorpion-Fish* I read it through and then double-read it. In other words, on the second reading I read each page twice before turning to the next. With just 30 lines a page and 140 pages, it didn't take long. It was entirely pleasurable and I felt I owed it to an author I'd once had breakfast with.

Initially I'd settled for a hurried skim. An hour later I'd returned to the contents page intrigued, unsettled and still not sure what sort of book it was. The narrative, in so far as it had one, was too surreal for a memoir, too static for a travelogue. Beginning with one departure, it ended with another, and not much happened in between. Where and when the not-much happened was also unclear. The setting had to be inferred. It was an unnamed island in the tropics but only the cover blurb identified it as Sri Lanka. The text made so little distinction between observation and hallucination that one couldn't be sure of anything. Nor were the characters any help, they being mostly insects. The one articulate exception, a levitating reprobate in tiny bootees and a clerical soutane, turned out to have died six years earlier. So far, so weird. But six years earlier than when? The chronology was as under-reported as the geography. In withholding even the most basic information, *The Scorpion-Fish* seemed intent on exploring the potential of the anti-travelogue.

This hadn't stopped reviewers from ranking its author along with

---

Nicolas Bouvier, *The Scorpion-Fish* (1981) · Trans. Robyn Marsack
Eland · Pb · 160pp · £12.99 · ISBN 9781780600444

Patrick Leigh Fermor as one of the twentieth century's finest travel writers. Born and often resident in Geneva, Bouvier wrote mostly in French, collected music, spent several years in Japan and succumbed to cancer in 1998. He was excellent company and, over our one breakfast, he'd explored the controversial idea that the Sandwich Islands were named for their abundance of breadfruit. That was in 1981, the year *Le Poisson-Scorpion* had been published; a year later it won the Prix des Critiques. The English translation by Robyn Marsack, then director of the Scottish Poetry Library, appeared soon afterwards. Yet at the time the uneasy sojourn described in the book already dated back more than a quarter of a century. After an erratic odyssey across Asia in a diminutive Fiat (described in *L'Usage du Monde*, 1963, *The Way of the World*: see *SF* no. 18), Bouvier had ended up spending nine months in what was still called Ceylon in 1955. He was a slow writer and, like Fermor, 'let a lot of water run under the bridge before returning to Ceylon's "negative enchantment"'. According to Ms Marsack, when he did finally revisit those nine months of 1955, it was with little enthusiasm or affection. He wrote 'in a trance fuelled by whisky and music'. Marsack calls it a case of 'writing as exorcism'. Confronting the scorpion-fish was 'something that had to be done, a painful analysis of what he regarded as a defeat, a slow loss of control over himself'.

Had I known all this at the start, I'd have been more sympathetic. A revealing quote from the novelist Louis-Ferdinand Céline – 'The worst defeat of all is to forget, especially what has crushed you' – should have alerted me, but instead of appearing on the first page it was reserved to the last. Likewise the translator's helpful Afterword, which follows it. I had missed both. It was mystification that prompted my second reading, and the elegance of the writing that ordained it be a double one.

Returning in a more suitable frame of mind, I stopped fussing over locations and directions to beach-bum, like Bouvier, round the fort area of what was evidently ex-colonial Galle. Getting the measure of his loping syntax and his sand-blasted imagery, I succumbed to the most devastating reverie I'd ever read. For all its peculiarities – and because of them – *The Scorpion-Fish* is one of those books that doesn't let go of you. Like an insistent dream, it dogs the waking day, challenging you to erase it or come up with something better. Either would be hard.

Take, for instance, the 'Oriental Patissery' which became Bouvier's favourite hang-out in his adopted island-home. 'It is worth reflecting', he begins, 'why, at 5 degrees latitude north, 77.5 degrees longitude east and 105 degrees in the shade, a shop selling nothing but curry fritters . . . should still think it necessary to stress that it's "oriental".' Does Brescia offer 'Western Shoe Repairs', he asks, or Bremen boast an 'Occidental Pantry'? 'As things stand, we are the ones who have imposed our manners, our measures, our meridians, our gods.' And our dialectics. The Patissery's clientele, a hapless group of 'academic ultranationalists', wore sarongs as a 'protest against western alienation, injured themselves once in a blue moon with their home-made bombs – of which they were the only victims – and gathered there each evening for their whist games'.

> Apostles without disciples, the group maintained a slightly tarnished virtue in lieu of a programme, and an astonishing ability to argue endlessly in the heat – getting themselves in trim for doctrinal quarrels with fraternal groups, for they were neither Stalinists, Maoists, Castroists nor Titoists but Trotskyites of more than twenty years' standing, no doubt the last ones . . . I felt that in the matter of ideology, as in business, we had once again palmed off old stock on them. If they were strongly attached to these outmoded goods it was because they had learned from experience that we wouldn't be back to collect them.

Equatorial Bolshevism was doomed anyway, like all other forms of social engagement below the Tropic of Cancer. It was just too hot.

Class struggle and the proletarian revolution were the inventions of an Arctic intelligentsia that 'blew on their fingers before writing'. 'Engels had a hot-water bottle, the proofs of *Kapital* were corrected in mittens, Trotsky's ink froze in the inkwell.' (But did they? Or was Bouvier improvising, as with the breadfruit?) Alone, mildly deranged and drawing heavily on dwindling resources – of cash, strength, memory – he had had much in common with the Trotskyites. He found their 'funereal hilarity' positively consoling.

> I am grateful to you, Soviet of the 'Oriental Patissery' [he recalled], and I see you again now: the oil lamp smokes and chars, a black icon; faces with large pores gleam in the night heat while time dissolves in ghostly speeches; through arak fumes you could cut with a knife the glow of a cheroot illuminates decayed teeth. They put down their cards, patiently poking at the past, as I did myself today. If you forbade the aged to use that little phrase 'do you remember', there would be no more conversation: we all have it in us to suddenly, quietly, cut our throats.

It was memories that moored one to the past and kept one sane. As each frayed and gave way, Bouvier slipped into deeper water and felt more alone and helpless than ever. Anyone trying to write who has shut themselves away in the back of beyond will know the feeling. His girl had just jilted him, his friends had left soon after he arrived, he knew no one and he was living on boiled fish-heads and arak. The Number One in the 1955 hit parade was 'Stranger in Paradise'. And he was suffering, explains Marsack, not just from acute self-awareness but from 'a triple attack of amoebiasis, malaria and jaundice'. Fever and the indiscriminate consumption of medicational drugs accounted for the light-headedness. Delirium followed, and then the hallucinations and visions.

One such was the levitating Father Alvaro in his absurd bootees and tatty soutane. Bouvier insists that, though Alvaro was indeed a ghost, he was a real ghost. Other people had met him; his distinguished career as a linguist and ethnographer was a matter of record; and thanks to Alvaro's editing, Bouvier's English-language journalism attained a 'mastery and sombre splendour' that were frankly miraculous. 'Twenty-five years later I cannot reread those texts without a shudder; they stink of sulphur and solitude.'

Whether the scorpion-fish also stank of sulphur and solitude is debatable. It too was real enough at first. A male with 'a sepia-flecked parasol of poisonous barbs', it lived in a jar on the counter of the local grocery store. The shop, a cavern draped with culinary oddities, was the domain of a Tamil Muslim so 'immobilized by her size' she never stirred from her accustomed sack of lentils. To repel intruders and to reach her stock of dried fish, spices and molasses she wielded a hooked stick. She was said to have a husband (Bouvier thought she might be sitting on him). She had two admirers, the fish and Bouvier.

> When she thinks herself alone, she leans her cheek against the glass [of the fish's jar] and makes faces at him, and he responds with generous quivering. I have found her at this game several times; I hold my breath and retreat on tip-toe, jealous as a discarded suitor. But there's no law against dreaming. If she ever surprised me spying, perhaps she would give me her mascot . . .

Sure enough, when in the book's last cathartic moments Bouvier vacates his garret in a ramshackle boarding-house, the fish is there on the shelf. So 'she did give it to me after all', he exclaims unconvincingly. Or maybe it's just the ghost of the fish. Blood is streaming down his face (in the darkness he'd collided with a signpost to the hospital) but the cut is as nothing to the 'tears of exhilaration and relief' that dribble into his packing. 'I began to revive: I had touched bottom, I was coming up like a bubble.'

Beside the jar he watched a little pink crab fold its claws 'in mourning', and 'in the nooks and crannies of my lodging I could see pincers, stings and wings, pointing'. For nine months the ants and termites had kept him company. He'd conversed with the cowardly cockroaches and been chided by an officious dung-beetle. Here the scorpion-fish in its glass jar would feel as excluded as he had. As the fever broke, and as the nightmare ended and the rains arrived, 'all my menagerie were wishing me an anxious farewell'.

> I left on the table the money I owed the landlord and for the last time looked round this blue attic where I'd been a prisoner so long. It was vibrating with ineffable music.

> The worst defeat of all is to forget,
> especially what has crushed you.

JOHN KEAY's latest book, *The Tartan Turban*, is a biography of Alexander Gardner, much of whose freebooting life was spent lost in Central Asia.

'Study to be quiet'

KEN HAIGH

I came to Winchester Cathedral to pay homage to one of my favourite authors. Not Jane Austen, though. I enjoy her work, but she doesn't need my support. When I arrive, a bevy of young admirers is already crouching over her foot-worn monument, striking poses and taking selfies with their smartphones. No, I have come to find the final resting place of Izaak Walton, author of *The Compleat Angler.*

I am directed to a tiny side chapel in the south transept – called Prior Silkstede's Chapel – where I find the writer pressed beneath a thick slab of black marble before the altar. Walton died on 15 December 1683, aged 90, and there is a pious, rather conventional poem carved on the stone, ending with the Latin tag: *Votis modestis sic flerunt liberi*, which I translate as 'This modest prayer his weeping children lament', revealing, perhaps, my lack of a classical education.

I have the chapel to myself this morning and settle on a rustic pew to admire the manner in which the rising sun sprays harlequinned light across the author's monument from the window above the altar. The stained glass is relatively new, installed in 1914, and erected in Walton's memory by admiring fishermen from Britain and America. My eye is drawn to the bottom right-hand corner of the window, where I spy Walton, dressed in a broad-brimmed hat, lace collar and high boots, quietly reading on the bank of the River Itchen with St Catherine's Hill rising in the background. He sits beneath the shade of a small tree, his rod, net and creel resting by his side. The scene is

---

Izaak Walton, *The Compleat Angler* (1653)
OUP · Pb · 336pp · £8.99 · ISBN 9780198745464

Anna Trench

captioned with his favourite quotation, taken from St Paul's first epistle to the Thessalonians, 'Study to be quiet', which is also the last line of his famous treatise on angling. Walton seems perfectly composed, and I wonder what he is reading. I clear my throat.

'Any luck?' I enquire, indicating the creel.

He looks up from his book and regards me with a gentle smile. 'No, not yet. But no day is spoiled that is spent fishing. For if I have not as yet caught a trout, my morning has not been wasted, for have I not had ample time for contemplation?'

'I suppose. Might you, um, have any profound thoughts to share?'

'I was thinking that the world is full of wonders and how it is man's lot to know so little of God's creation. For example, Pliny', he points to the book in his hand, 'is of the opinion that many of the flies with which we tempt the trout have their birth from a kind of dew that falls in the spring. The dew that falls on the leaves of trees breeds one kind of fly, that which falls upon flowers and herbs another, that on cabbages, yet another. In the same way, Gesner, who has written much on fishing, states that the pike, who is the tyrant of these waters, is bred by generation, as other fishes are, but may also spring spontaneously from the pickerel weed with the help of the sun's heat. Though men of science ponder these mysteries and others like them, I feel that we shall never plumb their bottom.'

I don't quite know what to say to this, so I change the subject. 'I saw some very nice trout in the Itchen yesterday. I'm surprised that there aren't more fishermen about.' I point to the meandering river winding out of sight beyond the frame of the window.

'This is private water. It belongs to the Bishop of Winchester, who is an old friend of mine. He is jealous of his privileges, and does not give permission easily.'

'Must be nice to be rich.'

'Nay, for the rich are always worried for coming of the next day. I would much rather be an angler, for do we not sit on cowslip banks, enjoy the cuckoo's song, and possess ourselves in as much quietness as this silver stream? I envy no man who eats better meat than I do, or who wears better clothes than I do, only him who catches more fish than I do.' He laughs. 'God never did make a more quiet, calm, innocent recreation than angling.'

'So I've read.'

He raises his eyes to the heavens and snaps his book shut. 'The noonday sun is passed. You will forgive me, but there are reaches of this river I wish to tempt before the afternoon is spent and I must return to my daughter's fireside.' He slips the book into his pocket and gathers up his fishing tackle. 'Remember, he that hopes to be a good angler must not only bring an inquiring, searching and observing wit, but he must bring a large measure of hope and patience to the art. Adieu.'

And with that he walks out of the frame.

*

Izaak Walton lived as an ironmonger in London until the English Civil War, when he closed his shop, took early retirement and moved to a small farm in the country near Shallowford in Staffordshire. There he began the book that would make him famous. *The Compleat Angler* is a scrapbook containing everything Walton knew about the pursuit of angling. It's hard to classify, for it contains fishing tips and bait recipes but also songs and poems and a spirited debate between a fisherman, a hunter and a falconer about the merits of each sport. (Of course, the fisherman wins the debate.) The first edition was published in 1653, two years after the Civil War ended, but he never really stopped working on it. New editions would continue to be published until his death. The final edition of 1676 was greatly expanded, and included an additional book written by his good friend Charles Cotton about the art of fishing with a fly for trout or grayling.

Walton spent the last forty years of his life writing and fishing in the company of like-minded friends, many of them clergy. He had close ties to the Church of England. His first wife had been the great-great-niece of Archbishop Cranmer, author of the English Book of Common Prayer. Walton's second wife was the stepsister of the Bishop of Bath and Wells. The poet John Donne was a close friend, for Donne was the vicar of St Dunstan-in-the-West in London when Walton was the verger and churchwarden there. In fact, after Donne's death, Walton would be asked to write a short biography of the poet, which proved so successful that he followed it up with a series of other pocket-sized biographies, most of them of prominent clergymen. As an old man, Walton would find a home in Farnham Castle as the guest of his friend George Morley, the Bishop of Winchester. Walton's daughter married the prebendary of Winchester Cathedral, and it was in her home that he would spend his final days.

The biggest myth surrounding Walton is the idea that he was a dedicated dry-fly fisherman. In fact, he was ecumenical in his fishing tastes. His book lists many methods of catching fish, including the use of live bait. Of the frog as an excellent bait for pike, he famously (or infamously) remarked, 'Use him as though you loved him, that is, harm him as little as you may possibly, that he may live the longer.' My favourite fishing tip is a bait recipe for coarse fish: 'You may make another choice bait thus: take a handful or two of the best and biggest wheat you can get, boil it in a little milk, like as frumity is boiled; boil it so till it be soft; and then fry it, very leisurely, with honey and a little beaten saffron dissolved in milk . . .' Sounds delicious. If I were a fish, I'm sure I would find this irresistible.

But the book is not *just* a manual for fishermen. It would hardly have stayed in print all these years if that's all it was; for *The Compleat Angler* is the most frequently reprinted book in English after the Bible. Angling, to Walton, represents an approach to life that is at once gentle, pious and reflective. When fishermen are accused of being simple, Walton's narrator, Piscator, replies:

> If by that you mean a harmlessness, or that simplicity which was usually found in the primitive Christians, who were, as most Anglers are, quiet men, and followers of peace; men that are simply wise, as not to sell their consciences to buy riches, and with them vexation and a fear to die; if you mean such simple men as lived in those times when there were fewer lawyers . . . then myself and those of my profession will be glad to be so understood.

Some readers have detected a hidden code in the book as well, where 'Angler' may be read as 'Anglican', where the virtues celebrated in fishermen are really the virtues Walton championed in Englishmen of a certain stripe; for at least one cause of the English Civil War was the desire of some sects to break free of the English Church, to abolish bishoprics and replace church hierarchy with a looser Presbyterian-style organization. Walton was an Anglican and a Royalist. He stood for tradition and received wisdom. But he was not a violent man. In fact, there is only one story which survives that portrays him as an active participant in the struggle, and it may be apocryphal. He is said to have once helped smuggle an important royal jewel, called the Lesser George, out of England to Charles II in exile.

Otherwise Walton led a retiring life, choosing to sit out the war and the Commonwealth in a quiet country backwater, spending his time writing and fishing. It is this gentle, good-natured man who comes across in the pages of *The Compleat Angler*, full of friendly advice, not all of it wise, and it is his lyrical celebration of pastoral life, with its cowslip banks and birdsong, its musical milkmaids and quiet country inns with their lavender-scented sheets, that we remember with such fondness.

KEN HAIGH is the author of *Under the Holy Lake: A Memoir of Eastern Bhutan.* He lives on the banks of the Beaver River in Ontario, Canada, where you might find him casting a fly during the trout season.

Sparkling Sydney

ELISABETH RUSSELL TAYLOR

The Wild Irish Girl, by Sydney Owenson, was first published in 1806, since when it has rarely been out of print. I knew nothing of this novel or its author until a few years ago, when I was writing about the Italian poet and philosopher Leopardi and needed to place this tormented genius against a real background. I read diaries and letters by those who took the Grand Tour and more than once came upon the name of one Lady Morgan, an Irish feminist and patriot who, by the age of 25, was supporting herself, her father and her sister on the novels, travel books, articles and pamphlets she wrote under her maiden name, Sydney Owenson.

As soon as I read Sydney on Italy I was hooked; I found her principled, cheerful, energetic, imaginative and decent: excellent company. She was passionate about her writing and regularly stuck at it for eight hours at a sitting. She had unusual confidence in herself and her femininity; she was creative – could make her own clothes and, when let down by her chef just a few hours before giving a dinner party, did the cooking herself. She believed in justice and equality at home and abroad which, like feminism and atheism, were not principles universally espoused by her contemporaries.

Unlike many travellers in the eighteenth and early nineteenth centuries, Sydney did not travel abroad to plunder her hosts of their art and artefacts but to familiarize herself personally with foreign places and peoples. She made an enormous impression wherever she went

---

Sydney Owenson, *The Wild Irish Girl* (1806)
OUP · Pb · 304pp · £8.99 · ISBN 9780199552498

and was courted and admired 'as well for her unrivalled talents as her elegant and unaffected manners'. Byron wrote of her *Italy* (1821): 'Her work is fearless and excellent . . . I know the country. I wish she had fallen in with me; I could have told her a thing or two that would have confirmed her position.' But of course she was roundly criticized too, by the usual suspects.

Before setting out, Sydney spent two years boning up on Italian history. She acquired a prodigious knowledge of the country's art and architecture, its social and political texture and the lie of the land. But it was her refreshingly personal reflections which most impressed me: 'enchanted' by the country and its people, she has a unique way of luring her readers to follow in her footsteps. She was a scholarly woman who nevertheless knew how to enjoy herself.

It is a great sorrow to me that in my old age I no longer have the strength to follow Sydney on her travels through Europe. In the past, when I became deeply affected by a book, I would set out to retrace the land and cityscapes – the reality in which it was set. This took me all over Europe, and solidified and intensified my memories. Today my journeys are confined to buses to and from the British Library, where writers more mobile than I do the footwork for me.

Getting about Italy during the early nineteenth century was uncomfortable – the roads unmade, the inns few and inhospitable and the food uneatable. Lady Morgan (her married name, under which she travelled) does not allow these trivialities to spoil her delight. As a tourist she leaves no church, no monument, no picture gallery, theatre, silkworm factory, university, library or public garden unvisited and unassessed. She attends the ballet, is loaned a box at the opera – normally 'set aside for the noblesse' – and a carriage. She is invited everywhere, and wherever she goes she writes up the scene as if she were painting it. But she does not allow what her eyes rejoice to see to blind her to the striking chasm between the stunning beauty and fecundity of the fields and the condition of the peasantry, who go 'bare-footed, dirty and slovenly'. As she moves across Italy she always has Ireland in mind, comparing the social injustices – the sheer waste of human life that she observes there – with those suffered in Ireland.

Buoyed up by what I found in the two heavy volumes of *Italy* (1821), I turned to Sydney's letters. They are unabashedly intimate, affectionate, informed and witty. I read her memoirs, from which I came to understand what made her both popular and controversial: she was a militant patriot; she was a feminist; she rejected religion. In addition, she was constantly exercised by the relationship between the oppressor and the oppressed. Her principal missions in life were to effect greater equality among people and to replace the view of Ireland and its people held by the English – ill-informed, ugly and patronizing – with her own.

Biographies refer to the excellent education Sydney's less educated father – a poor itinerant Catholic actor – had given his daughter. She had Latin and Greek, French and Italian, a taste for research and the ability to communicate her ideas clearly. But that education did not save her from having to earn her keep. The only way open to a woman of her age and social status was to get work as a governess and she made the most of this by storing up her experiences for future novels. She does not complain about being little more than a servant in the houses of the nobility, for she was loved by all upon whom she waited, regardless of the fact that not all her opinions tallied with theirs. It was through the patronage of her employers that she rose to become the most widely sought guest in London's and Dublin's most fashionable houses. Indeed, she was to become known as the 'Irish de Staël'.

The title her patrons negotiated for her doctor husband was not something which Sydney engineered, but it certainly helped her socially; as Lady Morgan she was always surrounded by people who wielded social, intellectual and political clout. No individual and no situation overawed or silenced her; she managed to maintain her own identity, upholding the virtues of old Ireland by dressing in medieval Irish costume and entertaining on the harp. She saw herself as belonging to a time when Irish language and literature flourished.

She was the first Irish writer to express the passion and commitment of those Anglo-Irish who took up the nationalist cause. At the same time, she preserved her femininity; she was admired for her looks and was clearly much occupied by her appearance. Though hardly what was deemed a great beauty – she was just four foot, chubby and 'quaint' – Sir Thomas Lawrence asked to be allowed to draw her. Sydney was clearly someone whose soul dominated. What started as affection and admiration for a woman quite unlike any other taking the Grand Tour ended by my reading *The Wild Irish Girl*.

The Wild Irish Girl is Sydney Owenson's manifesto, and her greatest success. It is an epistolary novel without much in the way of intricacies of plot, but with a purpose: to educate the English as to the real nature of the Irish and the history and culture of their ancient country. On the one hand, it is a fairy tale with fine descriptive writing. On the other, it is an allegory written at a time when the Irish seemed to have lost their identity. It tells of a prejudiced young Englishman, Horatio Mortimer, banished by his father to the family's Irish estates for his dissolute behaviour. His treatment of women has been gross, his financial dealings irresponsible and he has neglected his law studies. He has disgraced the family name.

The Mortimer family estates to which Horatio is banished had been won by conquest under Cromwell, since when things had gone from bad to worse for the Irish. From 1800 Ireland – through the Act of Union – had been a colony economically controlled by England. Sydney Owenson saw it as her responsibility to study ancient Gaelic history and culture, to set down the manifold sufferings of generations of Irish people and return to them an identity distinct from the English Protestants who had become their overlords.

Horatio has all the prejudices of the English of his time; he has never been to Ireland but believes – as do his contemporaries – that Ireland is a barbarous place inhabited by barbarous people. He compares what he does not know of the country to the 'savage desolations of Siberia'. He is sure that without educated company and refined entertainment he will be unbearably bored.

Arriving in Dublin, he is faced with all the 'vice, poverty, idleness and filth' he had expected, and finds the Irish 'dreadful and disgusting beyond all expression'. However, on leaving the city and heading north-west to the coast of Connaught, he starts to find himself unexpectedly touched by the pride, generosity and gratitude of the suffering populace he encounters, and he is captivated by the beauty of the Irish countryside:

> Mountain rising over mountain, swelled like an amphitheatre to those clouds which, faintly tinged with the sun's preclusive beams, and rising from the earthly summits where they had reposed, incorporated with the kindling aether of a purer atmosphere. All was silent and solitary – a tranquillity tinged with terror, or a sort of 'delightful horror', breathed on every side.

He is overwhelmed by what he sees, understanding through his encounters that the near-starving peasants huddled in hovels with their animals are the descendants of a noble people with a civilization much older than his own. Horatio is undergoing a moral education. He confronts the demolition of Ireland and the Irish brought about by the English, and on discovering that his own forebears benefited from Ireland's loss, sets about making amends.

I hope anyone inclined to get a copy of *The Wild Irish Girl* will be encouraged to find out more about Sydney and place her firmly in her rightful position as one of our most distinguished feminists. I do not imagine that if asked why she wrote, she would have disagreed with Orwell's answer to the same question: political purpose, historical impulse, aesthetic enthusiasm and sheer egoism.

ELISABETH RUSSELL TAYLOR is the author of six novels including the Virago Modern Classics *Pillion Riders* and *Mother Country*, and three collections of short stories. She lives in London and is currently writing her seventh novel.

First-rate Monsters

ANDREW NIXON

E. F. Benson's Mapp and Lucia books ruined Beethoven for me, and very nearly Shakespeare too.

Picture, if you will, the most appallingly pretentious person in the world: a well-dressed middle-aged lady at the piano, plonking her way through the slow first movement of the Moonlight Sonata. She is wearing her 'well-known Beethoven expression' with the 'wistfully sad far away look from which the last chord would recall her'. Her guests, enduring the entertainment in various attitudes of suicidal boredom, give dutiful little sighs as that last chord fades, and then steel themselves for . . . another rendition of the slow first movement of the Moonlight Sonata! For – though she pretends otherwise and that Beethoven composed the trickier second movement largely by mistake – it is in fact *the only tune she can play.*

This is Emmeline Lucas, aka 'Lucia', and I've not been able to enjoy the Beethoven sonata since meeting her. The Italian affectation of 'Lucia' is just that, since she has no connection with Italy and certainly doesn't speak the language. But by peppering her conversation with plenty of *mio caros* and *molto benes* she permits it to be thought that she is quite fluent in *la bella lingua*.

I'm afraid it gets worse. The bedrooms in Lucia's house have names like 'Othello' and 'Hamlet'. In the garden there is 'not a flower to

---

We can try to obtain second-hand copies of E. F. Benson's *Queen Lucia* (1920), *Miss Mapp* (1922), *Lucia in London* (1927), *Lucia's Progress* (1935) and *Trouble for Lucia* (1939). *Mapp and Lucia* (1931) is available as a Penguin paperback (304pp · £7.99 · ISBN 9780141187686).

be found save such as were mentioned in the plays of Shakespeare'. And the flowerbed beneath the dining-room window is known as 'Ophelia's border'.

In *Queen Lucia* (1920) this stellar snob lords it over the village of Riseholme, oppressing local society with her profound appreciation of Shakespeare, her merciless Moonlights, her smattering of Italian and her unrelenting energy. Then in *Lucia in London* (1927) she deploys these same weapons to conquer the capital.

Yes, Lucia is a ruthless social climber, a backstabber and a perfectly shameless pseud. But the funny thing is that, through the series of novels that follow, we the readers are generally on her side. And that's because a little distance away, in a picturesque East Sussex town, there lurks somebody far, far worse . . .

*

'Elizabeth was gazing out of the window with that kind, meditative smile which so often betokened some atrocious train of thought.'

From the garden room of Mallards, her ancestral home, the eponymous anti-heroine of *Miss Mapp* (1922) plots against her friends and neighbours. The garden room is important: it is a strategic vantage point affording clear views down the two principal streets of the town of Tilling, so she can chart all comings and goings in comfort.

Tilling is a lovely, chocolate-box sort of place, with cobbled streets and characterful houses inhabited by the archetypes of the interwar leisured class: vicar's wives, ageing spinsters, retired colonels. It is Elizabeth Mapp's great purpose to devise new and ingenious ways to make their daily lives slightly less pleasant than they would otherwise be, and to ensure that the round of garden parties and bridge evenings that is Tilling's social scene remains a hissing snake pit of envy and resentment.

The chief weapons in her armoury are thinly veiled sarcasm and cutting criticisms disguised as compliments. True, she is not the only culprit in the town's never-ending social war. The women of Tilling have, as one male character ruefully puts it, 'a pretty sharp eye for each other's little failings' (though the men are just as bad). But Mapp is by far the most ruthless and skilled operator. Hers are 'the most penetrating shafts, the most stinging pleasantries', and thus she is feared and admired by all.

Large and toothy, her face is 'corrugated by chronic rage and curiosity'. She terrifies local shopkeepers and tradesmen with continual niggling disagreements:

> Quarrelsome errands were meat and drink to Miss Mapp: Tuesday morning, the day on which she paid and disputed her weekly bills, was as enjoyable as Sunday mornings when, sitting close under the pulpit, she noted the glaring inconsistencies and grammatical errors [in the sermon].

In short, she is a master of what we might now call 'passive-aggressive' behaviour: never quite saying anything unambiguously insulting, but still making sure that everyone in the room feels jolly uncomfortable.

Like Lucia, Mapp is a first-rate monster, vivid and fully realized. Had their creator, E. F. Benson, left off at *Miss Mapp*, he might still have earned a respectable middling position in the pantheon of English observational comedies. But, fortunately, he hit upon the one indisputably great idea of his career, which was to elevate him to the top rank and preserve his name for posterity: he brought his two monsters together.

If you are a first-time reader of E. F. Benson, I urge you to start with *Miss Mapp* and the two 'solo' Lucia novels and work your way towards *Mapp and Lucia* (1931), rather than diving straight into the most famous volume in the series. The steadily growing prospect of these two titanic female egos meeting each other is quite thrilling, and conjures thoughts of unstoppable forces and immovable objects.

The wheeze Benson cooks up is that Lucia – newly widowed but with her chaste companion Georgie in tow – comes to Tilling to rent

Elizabeth Mapp's house for the summer. The latter doesn't leave town: an eccentric local tradition sees the residents all holidaying in each other's homes, meaning that Mapp is ever available to 'pop in' with helpful advice, to keep an eye on how her beloved Mallards is being mistreated, and generally to try to 'run' Lucia in the Tilling social scene.

Alas, she soon finds that her tenant is not the sort of person who can easily be run. ('I see I must be a little firm with her,' thought Lucia, 'and when I've taught her her place, then it will be time to be kind.') Worse, Lucia emerges as a clear threat to Mapp's position as dictator of Tilling. She trumps Mapp's teas with dinner parties, turns her own Mallards against her by hosting lavish garden parties and beats the locals into submission with the Moonlight.

Hostilities commence early and escalate rapidly. Mapp fires her most stinging pleasantries; Lucia combats them with retorts of 'paralysing politeness'. Before long they are locked in a deadly war of attrition with first one then the other gaining the upper hand. The war doesn't let up through the rest of the novel or the sequels, *Lucia's Progress* (1935) and *Trouble for Lucia* (1939).

These three books are masterpieces of social satire and a joy to read. They're vicious and gripping and wickedly funny, and they remain so after repeated rereading. They're also about as deep as a puddle.

*

Posterity is a curious thing. Edward Frederic ('Fred') Benson (1867–1940) was, from one angle, a rather frivolous odd-man-out in a very serious literary family. His father was a giant of the Victorian age: the domineering, humourless Edward White Benson, first Headmaster of Wellington College, first Bishop of Truro (where he invented the Christmas service of Nine Lessons and Carols) and later Archbishop of Canterbury. Fred's elder brother Arthur was Master of Magdalene College, Cambridge, and a heavyweight essayist and

EFB in his thirties

prolific diarist who composed the lyrics to 'Land of Hope and Glory'. Their younger siblings Robert Hugh and Margaret were respectively a pioneer of dystopian fiction and a celebrated Egyptologist. Literature simply poured out of the Bensons. At Christmas their favourite parlour game was to write pastiches of each other's work. Fred himself published close to a hundred books in all conceivable genres from ghost stories and memoirs to sporting history, by way of serious fiction. Yet of all the countless millions of these combined Benson-written words, almost nothing is still read today except *Mapp and Lucia.*

The young Fred would have been appalled at such a legacy. Much of his literary life was spent trying to write something weighty enough to escape the shadow of his own first novel. *Dodo* (1893) – a sensational, smash-hit melodrama about a social climber – was openly disdained by his father and elder brother. In pursuit of gravitas he published several important works on archaeology as well as biographies of Sir Francis Drake and Charlotte Brontë. But try as he might, in the public mind Fred remained the creator of the eponymous Dodo . . . until he came up with the even more outrageous social climber Lucia. For all his efforts he was destined to be remembered for a handful of comedies of middle-class manners.

Then again, from another angle Fred's achievement is admirable, even triumphant. There was a dark side to the Bensons. The patriarch Edward White had proposed to his cousin Mary Sidgwick ('Minnie') when he was in his mid-twenties and she was just 11 years old. Their weird, virtually arranged marriage took place six years later. The tensions within the family were awful. Of the six children Minnie bore, one died and at least three suffered from severe mental illness. None produced offspring of their own; they were almost certainly all non-practising homosexuals (as indeed was Minnie: after she was widowed she happily cohabited and shared a bed with Lucy Tait, daughter of the previous Archbishop of Canterbury). Arthur was plagued by manic-depressive psychosis, Robert Hugh had a catastrophic entanglement with the notorious fraudster Frederick Rolfe ('Baron Corvo') and Margaret ended her days in the Priory after succumbing to a 'violent homicidal mania'.

Throughout all this, Fred led a remarkably sanguine and benevolent existence. In contrast to his insular siblings he was sociable and well-rounded. He was a gifted sportsman, spending his winters ice-skating to championship standard and his summers relaxing on the island of Capri. He knocked out bestselling books without much apparent effort. In the last part of his life Fred settled in the East Sussex town of Rye, eventually becoming the town's mayor and living in Lamb House, the former home of his friend Henry James. From there he quietly, selflessly gave emotional succour and financial support to the suffering Arthur and Margaret.

And, of course, he fictionalized Lamb House as 'Mallards' and Rye as 'Tilling' and populated them with a cast of unforgettable caricatures, of whom Mapp and Lucia are merely the most vivid. Others include the camp bachelor Georgie Pillson, with his daring trousers and precious cabinet of 'bibelots'; the Reverend Bartlett who, despite hailing from Birmingham, talks in 'a mixture of faulty Scots and spurious Elizabethan English'; and the Bohemian artist 'Quaint' Irene, who wears men's clothes and is always doing preposterous arty things ('she sat for half an hour at Lucia's piano, striking random chords and asking Lucia what colour they were'). Far from feeling insulted by these parodies, it seems that the locals of Rye were all eager to claim credit as their models.

While the rest of the wider Benson canon slides deeper into obscurity, Tilling remains in rude health. Various novelists have written follow-ups, a Friends of Tilling Society counts Gyles Brandreth and Alexander McCall Smith among its patrons and is active on Twitter, while a terrific BBC adaptation was made as recently as 2014.

In the Mapp and Lucia books Fred Benson's prose is effortlessly entertaining. The satire is clear-eyed, drained of any delusion about human nature, but not entirely unforgiving. Above all else, it is very, very funny. His command of twisty witticisms ('paralyzing politeness', 'vindictive forgiveness') is second only to Wilde; his construction of farcical situations in which middle-class snobs get their comeuppance, second only to Wodehouse. As a dissector of the timeless human qualities of bitchiness, cattiness and vacuous viciousness he is quite without peer.

For as long as there is society and snobbery there will be Lucias and Mapps. They are, therefore, probably immortal. Posterity is a curious thing, but perhaps Fred Benson's legacy isn't such a bad one in the end. It's just a shame I can't listen to the Moonlight Sonata any more.

ANDREW NIXON is a writer from Bristol, and the co-founder of *The Dabbler*.

Word from the Wood

GALEN O'HANLON

My grandfather taught me how to light a fire. I remember crouching by his side in the sitting-room on cold mornings, watching his huge hands crunching the paper, piling up the kindling, slotting the logs into place and lighting a match.

After the flare of the match, a few moments of silence. Then a glow, a flicker, a thin tongue of flame curling at the paper's edge, sliding up a length of kindling, touching the bark, then slipping back into the little cave of orange light in the middle of the pile. It was my job to watch it didn't go out, while he went to see to the cows. I crouched, and watched.

There's an essay in Aldo Leopold's *A Sand County Almanac* (1949) that brought me back to that moment:

> My dog does not care where heat comes from, but he cares ardently that it come, and soon. Indeed he considers my ability to make it come as something magical, for when I rise in the cold black pre-dawn and kneel shivering by the hearth making a fire, he pushes himself blandly between me and the kindling splits I have laid on the ashes, and I must touch a match to them by poking it between his legs.

It's one of those times when a book transports you instantly into a memory: conjuring the feelings, the smells, the sounds of a brief, vivid moment of childhood. I was there again, with my grandfather,

---

Aldo Leopold, *A Sand County Almanac, and Sketches Here and There* (1949)
OUP · Pb · 240pp · £8.99 · ISBN 9780195007770

but this time feeling very much like the dog that Leopold describes: silent, expectant.

A Sand County Almanac, and Sketches Here and There is a collection of Leopold's writing from the 1930s and 1940s. Author, scientist, ecologist, forester, conservationist and environmentalist, Leopold was truly a powerhouse of natural history. His *Sand County* had a profound impact on the environmental movement, introducing the idea of wilderness management and environmental ethics. That makes it all sound rather dry, but in fact the essays sparkle with precise details. Whether he's picking out the order of birdsong at dawn in a Wisconsin wood, following a mink track through the snow in January or tracing the first signs of thaw in spring, the essays are warm, beautiful things. They have some of the aphoristic appeal of Emerson, the wildness of Thoreau, the poetry of Whitman – but it's the rhythm of them that gets you. Here he is in 'March', having heard the honk of geese overhead, ruminating on the role their migration plays in the world:

> By this international commerce of geese, the waste corn of Illinois is carried through the clouds to the Arctic tundras, there to combine with the waste sunlight of a nightless June to grow goslings for all the lands in between. And in this annual barter of food for light, and winter warmth for summer solitude, the whole continent receives as net profit a wild poem dropped from the murky skies upon the muds of March.

This is typical of Leopold's style. His broad brushstrokes cover many thousands of miles to paint this grand pattern in nature, and then focus on a single detail – that wild poem, there to be enjoyed by anyone who knows how to stop and listen.

These essays are absorbing stories – and they are useful too. We learn about the draba, a tiny flower that's the first to bloom on the prairie, and about the sky dance of the woodcock in April and May; we learn about the owl at dawn who 'in his trisyllabic commentary,

plays down the story of the night's murders'. And we learn to see things from every viewpoint ('at this time every year I wish I were a musk rat, eye-deep in the marsh', he says). So we see the woods as a dog sees them: a landscape of smells, full of rabbits. And we see them as a rabbit does, with a keen sense of the quickest line from meadow to woodpile hideout, for when the dog comes. Leopold teaches us how to read the stories in animal ecology, how to fit the tiniest momentary detail into a much bigger narrative of landscape and nature.

This idea of the natural world as a book to be read runs throughout Leopold's essays. In 'February', he ties together the chopping of wood with the making of history: 'from each year the raker teeth pull little chips of fact, which accumulate in little piles, called sawdust by woodsmen and archives by historians'. The essay starts with Leopold looking at the fire he's made with wood that he's cut from an old oak on his farm. From there he traces time back from the log to the wood to the tree, and follows the saw as it cuts through eighty rings, slicing through eighty years of American history as it goes.

> Now our saw bites into the 1920s, the Babbittian decade when everything grew bigger and better in heedlessness and arrogance – until 1929, when stock markets crumpled. If the oak heard them fall, its wood gives no sign . . . In March 1922, the 'Big Sleet' tore the neighboring elms limb from limb, but there is no sign of damage to our tree. What is a ton of ice, more or less, to a good oak?
>
> Rest! Cries the chief sawyer, and we pause for breath.

The words carry the rhythm of the saw, back and forth through the tree, through time. That rhythm carries through each repetition of 'Rest! Cries the sawyer . . .' – and the whole piece builds into a grand picture of the world as witnessed by the oak. In less skilled hands this might be a tortuous extension of a metaphor, but the strength and balance of Leopold's prose are mesmerizing – much like watching the flames of a fire.

Leopold is a master at seeing things differently. Whether he takes on the perspective of a goose or a mink or a muskrat, he creates these vivid worlds from the animals he has observed. But it is more than a clever prose style. One of his most famous pieces, 'Thinking like a Mountain', describes a moment when there is a deep shift in his thought. He kills a wolf, thinking that a land without wolves would be the deer hunter's paradise. But as he watches the 'fierce green fire die in her eyes' he sees something new: that the wolf is integral to the life of the mountain, a keystone species on which the health of everything else depends. Having seen the devastation by deer of all wild country without wolves, he comes to think that 'just as a deer herd lives in mortal fear of its wolves, so does a mountain live in mortal fear of its deer'. Projects to reintroduce wolves to places like Yellowstone National Park have shown what he meant, and led to the latest thinking on the possibilities of restoring land to its original state of wilderness.

From their focus on the ecology of a single small farm in Wisconsin, the essays work towards an ethics of land: 'The Upshot'. This final section of the book is Leopold's concerted effort to set out a way in which we might negotiate the relationship of humans to land. All the work that Leopold does in the first two sections – demonstrating how to think like a beaver, a burr oak or a grebe – is now put to use in changing the role of Homo sapiens from one of conqueror of the land community to a fellow citizen and inhabitant of it. It's a compelling case, even if it seems that what he really wants is impossible: he'd like there to be fewer people on the planet.

Many scientists and ecologists and writers have built on the foundations that Leopold laid down in *A Sand County Almanac*, but that's not the real reason the book has lasted. The secret of its appeal lies in the natural rhythms of life in its pages. To read these essays is to sit once again with a grandfather, to learn the lost wisdom of the woodsman, to appreciate the ancient warmth of a fire, to read the wealth of detail in a small patch of earth, and to follow your nose along a skunk track, carved by his smooth belly in the deep January snow.

GALEN O'HANLON is a writer in Newcastle upon Tyne. He thinks about his grandfather every time he lights a fire.

Grandmother's Footsteps

CECILY BLENCH

My grandmother lived to the age of 101, but for me what defined her most were the years she spent in India during the Second World War. As a child I plagued her with questions about this exotic interlude, made all the more remarkable by the air of quiet conventionality that she exuded in later life.

In the sitting-room of her small house in the town where I was born, her white hair carefully curled, she passed round biscuits and poured tea, stirring gently with a silver teaspoon as she asked me about school, then college, then university. It was hard to imagine that she had once been my age, and that two years later at the age of 28 she had boarded a ship headed east, and said goodbye to her family for the foreseeable future.

She was born in the winter of 1914, just as the first war was beginning, to a family of prosperous farmers in Worcestershire. I had long assumed that it was the second war that had jolted her out of her provincial existence, but I was wrong. She told me that by the late 1930s she had already done her training as a nurse and in fact was planning to go west, to the prairies of the United States, where nurses were in short supply. She would have travelled between towns on horseback, dispensing medicine and bandages to grateful pioneer folk. 'It all sounded terribly romantic!' she said, smoothing the napkin on her lap.

Angela Bolton, *The Maturing Sun: An Army Nurse in India, 1942–1945* (1986), published by the Imperial War Museum, is now out of print, but we can look for second-hand copies.

But then the war came, and immediately it was clear that she was needed elsewhere. The nurses on the troopship going east were unsure where they were headed, but when the news came through that Singapore had fallen they knew that India was their destination.

India! The story of her time there was told in snippets. She had to be pressed to recall significant events, although she would occasionally mention, offhand, an anecdote about her experiences, through which I built up a vague timeline. The main facts of the matter were these. She had worked as a nurse in India for almost four years, in several locations including Assam, distinguishing herself as a hard worker in the most gruelling of conditions. Near the end of the war she had married my grandfather, a shy but evidently brave army officer, in Calcutta Cathedral.

I tried to get her to tell me more, but she was reluctant to waste time talking about the past when there was gardening to be done, or church to attend, or one of the many causes she cared about to be supported. She was a flurry of activity, and she only really slowed down in the last two or three years of her life.

When she died in January 2016, despite my sadness I felt two overwhelming and unexpected emotions. One was a feeling of 'rightness'. A woman who had lived so well and so fully had left us at exactly the right time. She was still living in her own home; she was not ill; she was, so far as we knew, content. The end of her life was a better end than most people are granted. She was tired, and she had a cup of tea, and she went to sleep.

The other feeling was an urge to continue what I had started, and learn more about her. My uncle had told me of a memoir by a woman called Angela Bolton who had nursed in India at the same time as Grandma. *The Maturing Sun* (1986) is not a long book or a work of great literature, but it is a compelling portrait of nursing life during the war. I found a second-hand copy and began to read. I was less than halfway through when, six months after she'd left us, Grandma strolled on to the page.

This is where she appears for the first time, in Calcutta:

> On leaving the Grand Hotel next morning I ran into Sister Copping, the rosy-cheeked, dark-haired girl from Yorkshire who had sung 'Linden Lea' on the *Monarch of Bermuda.* With her was the blonde, extremely shy Mary King, who I thought had the most beautiful face of all the women on the ship, yet who shrank from any social gathering.

Mary King was Grandma.

I always thought that exclaiming 'Oh!' was something that only happened in books, but I actually did it, so amazed and moved was I by her sudden appearance. I felt for a moment that I had got her back. Then, as I carried on reading, she reappeared with increasing regularity.

Mary King next pops up in Assam, where she and Angela Bolton worked in the same hospital for a few months. The duties of the Indian hospital servants are listed, and there they suddenly are, cutting the lawn 'with a pair of scissors borrowed from Mary King's sewing box'. So much comedy and mystery in that story! Did Grandma know they had 'borrowed' her scissors? I thought of how horrified she would have been if she had found me or my sister Daisy using a precious pair of sewing scissors to trim the grass.

A little later the author finds herself working with Mary King in the midst of a cholera epidemic at the hospital. The ten patients entrusted to their care survive, and Angela observes:

> The normally silent Mary King came to life over this traumatic episode, revealing depths of feeling that I for one had not known existed in her. Behind that calm face with its perfect features dwelt a personality that slept like a *princesse lointaine*, waiting to be awakened by the right circumstances or person into a joyous vitality. I hoped that I would be around to see it happen.

I had been prepared for Grandma to be mentioned only briefly in the book, or to be described unfavourably, but this kind and perceptive view of her personality made me feel quite affectionate towards Angela Bolton. Grandma *could* be frosty, I had always known that – the same shyness that my mother and I also suffer from and which is often mistaken for snobbishness or aloofness.

Two pages later, 'Mary King took her mysterious self to an unknown destination' and I worried for a moment that that was the last of her. I had a feeling, though, that the author of the book would not let me down.

Mary King's last appearance comes in July 1945, when Angela travels to Calcutta to see a man called Teddy whom she loves but isn't sure whether to marry. In the end Angela breaks it off with Teddy and goes out for a cheering dinner at the Grand Hotel with a fatherly brigadier:

> While I was combing my hair and renewing my lipstick in the cloakroom halfway through the evening, who should enter but Mary King, back at the BMH, Calcutta, once more. She looked a different person from the retiring, self-effacing beauty with the detached expression I remembered; her sleepy blue eyes were wide and alert, and she greeted me with an enthusiasm I had never known before. It did not take me long to spot the cause of the transformation. I saw that she was wearing a diamond ring on her left hand. She told me that she had just become engaged and was at the Grand with her fiancé to celebrate. I was so pleased that I gave her a hug and a kiss, a thing I would never have dared to do in the past.

Angela's story continues (for the record she lived happily ever after) but Grandma's part in this tale is complete as she waltzes, one supposes, out of the cloakroom at the Grand Hotel, Calcutta, to rejoin my grandfather, who is waiting for her at a candlelit table. Ahead of them lie laughter and love. They will go trekking in the

This photo of Mary King, signed by her, was probably sent to her fiancé during their engagement

Himalayas on their honeymoon while the war is still on. After it's over they'll go back to England for the birth of their first child, my mother, before being posted to Germany and, later, Malaya. Grandma will raise five children in army houses and uncomplainingly uproot her family time and again.

There will also be tragedy and despair – my grandfather, by this time a major in the SAS, will die in action in Borneo less than twenty years later, still in his early forties, and Grandma will have to pick up the fragments of her life. But she will rise from the ashes magnificently, never remarrying but loving her children and grandchildren fiercely, working hard to help the less fortunate at the Citizens Advice Bureau and the mental health charity Mind, and always taking pleasure in her garden. She will be respected and loved and will live a long and fulfilling life, eventually departing the world as gracefully as she had lived in it.

But all that is to come. For now she is young and in love. *The Maturing Sun* provides a few glorious snapshots of Grandma's time in India, and a glimpse of the experiences that shaped the rest of her life. I am infinitely grateful to Angela Bolton for including my grandmother in her own fascinating memoir. I cried while reading it, but laughed as well, recognizing Grandma in this portrayal – frosty, beautiful and loving. What a treat, so soon after losing her, to find her again.

CECILY BLENCH works for a small publisher in London and is currently writing a travel book about Burma, as well as making notes for a travel-biography of her grandmother.

Bibliography

Blowing Our Own Trumpet!

'Dear Slightly Foxed, I don't usually write these things but I wanted to contact you to let you know how much I love your publication. Each issue adds two or three books to my to-be-read list, which it doesn't particularly need but my soul does.'
N. Edwards, Leicestershire

'I just have to let you know that right now, under the Christmas tree with the quarterly and a range of *SF* books, I am so grateful for the existence of *SF*. In the midst of some rough life-weather this moment just makes me very happy and content. Thank you so much for all the work you do. It brightens up life.'
M. van Dijk, The Netherlands

'You people deserve a medal for being benefactors to humanity – shining lights in a dark and dreadful world.'
R. Dingle, Devon

Coming Attractions

URSULA BUCHAN joins Richard Hillary at Fighter Command · RICHARD HOLLOWAY finds redemption in art · WILLIAM PALMER examines Zeno's conscience · KATE JONES falls for A. L. Barker · ADAM FOULDS discovers England with the poet Geoffrey Hill · JANE FEAVER remembers life at Faber & Faber · ANTHONY LONGDEN enjoys the work of an irreverent Reverend · DAISY HAY returns to the Chalet School

15% OFF
RUDYARD
KIPLING TITLES
RUDYARD KIPLING
KIM

FS
The Folio Society